JESUS *Wept*

COLIN CLARK

ISBN 978-1-64079-743-7 (Paperback)
ISBN 978-1-64079-744-4 (Digital)

Christian Faith Publishing, Inc.
296 Chestnut Street
Meadville, PA 16335
www.christianfaithpublishing.com

Printed in the United States of America

CONTENTS

ACKNOWLEDGMENTS

To God who is the author of all wisdom. "*But if any of you lacks wisdom, let him ask of God, who gives to all generously and without reproach, and it will be given to him*" (James 1:5). I want to thank God for letting me put my name on something He wrote.

To Jesus who spoke the most underrated phrase in all of history. "*Therefore when Jesus had received the sour wine, He said, 'It is finished!' And He bowed His head and gave up His spirit*" (John 19:30).

To the Holy Spirit who rushes to our weaknesses with comfort and healing. "*And suddenly there came from heaven a noise like a violent rushing wind, and it filled the whole house where they were sitting. And there appeared to them tongues as of fire distributing themselves and they rested on each one of them. And they were all filled with the Holy Spirit and began to speak with other tongues, as the Spirit was giving them utterance*" (Acts 2:2–4).

To my wife, Janelle, who has lovingly supported without question, *every* endeavor I have ever conceived. She unselfishly loves God, family, and life in that order, and her prayers have pulled me back from the abyss more times than I could possibly be aware of.

To Pastor Jerry Dickinson of the West Side Church of God in Glendale, Arizona, who came alongside me with his passion for God and changed my life.

FOREWORD

Well-published authors likely have numerous reasons for writing their books; I have one. ***I believe Christians are not getting the full value from Christ's suffering on the cross.*** In fact, we have barely scratched the surface of the blessings that are available to us. How dismaying this must be to our Lord. Despite all the pain, anguish, and suffering from the diseases He bore; the burden and evil from all the sin that He endured; and most of all, the rejection He felt—not by us—but by His Father who had to turn away from Him when He was on the cross—despite all of these things, we Christians have failed to fully grasp grace and failed to manifest the blessings available to us.

Ask yourself—that's right—stop reading a minute and ask yourself, *"Do I have the joy that the Bible talks about? Or do I have anxieties and worries? Do I have a good prayer life? If you, or someone close to you was diagnosed with a life-threatening disease, do you have confidence that being in the presence of Jesus through prayer would give you a favorable resolution as it did during New Testament times?"*

The next obvious question would be, "*Have you had times in the past when your prayers were NOT answered?*"

As a pastor licensed in 2008 by the Church of God, Anderson, Indiana, I have been in contact with countless numbers of people going through seasons of distress, disillusionment, and distrust. Some of these people are mentioned in *Jesus Wept*. I am part of that group, and my intent is to share with you what God shared with me; how He taught me in the midst of my greatest trial to rest in Him and find healing and peace. If you are wondering where God is and why He isn't answering your prayers, this book will change your life and give you the answers you seek.

All biblical references are found in the New American Standard Bible. I started to write *Jesus Wept* in the fall of 2012, but it wasn't until early 2014 that God showed me the mysteries that had always eluded me.

I am an inquisitive individual; never content with surface or shallow answers. Faith requires simplicity; unfortunately, yet in many ways thankfully, I have always challenged God for more wisdom, more answers, and more complexity. I've had a lot of "Yeah, buts" and "Why is it, Lord…?" in my spiritual walk.

I have a bachelor of arts degree from the University of New Hampshire, a degree in accounting from McGill University in Montreal, Quebec, Canada and a Canadian CPA, which is called a CA or Chartered Accountant earned while I was apprenticing at Coopers & Lybrand in Montreal.

I have worked in and associated with the peoples of Canada, the United States, Belgium, France, Italy, Japan, and South Korea. I played ice hockey in college and met with the Montreal Canadiens of the National Hockey League to pursue a professional career in hockey but decided to go for my CA instead. While working for three years in Japan, I joined a local hockey team in Kyoto. I have also played semipro baseball and fast-pitch softball in Canada.

I began studying music when I was eight and even now can feel a cold sweat coming over me as I remember my piano teacher, Madame Vagara, rapping my knuckles with her ruler. I taught myself classical guitar during my stay in Japan. I sang in church choirs; played church organ and piano, as well as keyboards in church contemporary worship groups; and led worship in several churches—wherever there was a need.

I have pastored churches in temporary situations and led many Bible studies not only in church but also at my place of employment.

I am telling you all of this to reveal to you the many paths I have taken and the many different personalities, both in and out of country, I have mingled with. There's nothing you are going through that I have not seen or addressed before. Does that sound smug? It's not. It's been hard work for the most part. There have been language and cultural issues to deal with; people who mistrusted me and those who were way too macho or savvy to want to hear the "Good News".

If you are a new Christian, you may feel that this book is too deep for you, as I use Bible verses constantly to illustrate my points. Don't give up on this. Instead, let me share this personal tidbit to encourage you:

Several years before, I decided to present myself to our church denomination's credentials committee to start the journey of becoming licensed, my pastor at the time, Jerry Dickinson, West Side Church of God in Glendale, Arizona, requested that he and I do a weekly Bible study. I was leading worship in the traditional/blended service and to be honest with you, I really didn't see the need for a weekly one-on-one with him. After all, I had accepted the Lord *twenty-four years earlier*! Keep this in mind as you read on.

He would ask me to turn to a scripture in the Old Testament, and I had no idea where to look. I felt foolish and embarrassed. I started holding my thumb in the index so I could turn to it first and get a page number.

Then he would say to me, "*Well, brother Clark, what's God been saying to you this week?*" "***What?*** You're kidding, right? What's God been saying to me? I don't know! He hasn't been saying anything to me!"

Well, that silence was embarrassing too. You know what I learned to do? During my thirty-minute drive to see him, I would think up topics to offer as evidence that God was talking to me or laying things on my heart. He never questioned me and to this day, I don't know if I fooled him or not. But something else happened during all of that deceit. I noticed how godly he was. I began to realize that when I was in His presence, I felt like I was in the presence of God also. And I wanted more. I wanted to know as much as he knew; I wanted to spend more of my time in the presence of God, and in time, I wanted to become a pastor!

If you are a seasoned Christian, I hope to offer you some things that you may not have thought about. For example, "*Stop asking for God's will to be done at the end of your prayers.*" Or do you know "*your prayers release evil?*" Finally, I might challenge you "*to undergo an identity shift when you are interceding for someone.*"

If you are just beginning your Christian walk, this book will give you a foundation of encouragement, a treasure trove of truths to keep the enemy's attacks at bay and a mountain of comfort in the knowledge that God loves you—dearly!

For me, the most important thing I will try to teach you is that ***prayer is not about asking, it's about receiving***.

1

It's All about You!

If I'd had my way, I would have called this book the same as I called the original Bible study—***Behind Enemy Lines***. I had often heard the expression "*there are no atheists in foxholes*," suggesting that having an enemy not only staring you down, but also pinning you down, would cause everyone at some point to reach out for help to a higher power. After all, that's the purpose of this book—*to promote prayer*. But I began to toy with the title and even had others play with it until finally, I had about fifty alternatives, none of which I liked or made any sense. The original title appealed to me because we *are* surrounded by Satan and his evil schemes. By then however, in my consternation over choosing a title, I had prayed and asked God what title He wanted. Hence, *Jesus Wept*.

The most important thing you need to know in your Christian walk is how much God loves you. A mighty God, author of all creation, weeps over the condition of a few who had gathered to mourn the death of Lazarus. This event, recorded in John 11:35, should be your assurance that you aren't lost in the astronomical numbers of human souls that have existed since day one. That's why the Bible speaks of God knowing the number of hairs on your head; or knowing, naming, and placing every star in the heavens. God isn't a small God looking after a few things. He's a big God looking after immense numbers of things. He's very capable of knowing who you are and of loving you.

A Comparison between Godly Care and Human Care

There's a story about Napoleon Bonaparte, French emperor and military leader in the early 1800s, visiting his troops in outlying battle grounds. He would speak with the local military commanders about certain men before reviewing the troops. Then when he walked down the line, he would stop at each of the men he had learned about and ask them intimate questions about their families. He not only knew the soldier's name but the names of his parents, wife, and children as well. Later in their barracks, the selected men would be ecstatic that their respected leader knew about them. "See," they would share, "he knows who we are! He cares about us! Vive la France! Let us have our victory!"

Unlike Napoleon, who learned of a few soldiers in order to impress many; God knows all of us but unfortunately seems to impress only a few. God knows every minute detail about our lives. One of the pastors I served under was addressing in his sermon certain reasons why people don't pray, and one of them was that the issue was "too small to bother God with." He about came out of his shoes; "Are you nuts?" he asked rhetorically, "everything's small to God!"[1]

Jesus Wept will not only give you new perspectives on prayer but will show why you can know and have confidence that God cares about you. It's hard to have faith in a God we know so little about; and without faith, James 1 tells us, "*But he must ask in faith without any doubting, for* ***the one who doubts*** *is like the surf of the sea, driven and tossed by the wind. For that man* ***ought not to expect that he will receive anything from the Lord***" (James 1:6–7; emphasis mine).

Listen, folks, these are hard times. The unrest in the Arab world is unsettling enough, but we have major problems right here in the States. Of course, a pastor would tell you to pray; but God showed me that if His children are to survive today's world of violence and unrest; the frustration of political inactivity, stalemate, and uncertainty; the increasing unemployment and debt levels; the tragedy of people losing their homes and the rising levels of anxiety and subsequent health concerns—if people are to survive all of these, the first thing they need to learn is how much God loves them and how much they can trust Him to walk them through it all.

Many will scoff at the idea that prayer can bring change—change to their position in life; change to their health; change to their powerful government (a kind of "you can't fight city hall" approach). But such pessimisms are not supported biblically. Of course, the world would be pessimistic and urge you not to be foolish and leave your life to prayer. But the real authority—the Bible—tells a far different story.

The entire book of Judges in the Old Testament tells of the oppressive, horrible conditions of the Israelites after entering the promised land. The people were far from thankful to God for His blessings after leading them out of slavery in Egypt and setting them up in Palestine. They fell away from loving and worshipping God and chaos followed. Their life cycle can be summed up as follows: ***Israel is sinful, worshipping idols; Israel is enslaved by various invasions; Israel cries out to God to help them; God delivers a judge or a prophet among them who restores calm and peace; for a time Israel worships the Lord***. This cycle repeats itself *nine times*! Every time, God is faithful and brings strong leadership to them, restoring their way of life, bringing peace. And nine times, they fall away from God. Don't tell me that God doesn't hear our cries, doesn't forgive us, and doesn't bless us. We're the unfaithful ones!

Your fail-safe position (your plan B, your golden parachute or whatever it's called these days) for survival and peace of mind is ***not*** your job, your family, your bank account, your education, or your ego. Get over yourself and realize that the whole world is trying to do what you are trying to do. And if that's the case, then what has changed? Isn't that the way it always is, except now, the intensity level, the stakes are higher?

Instead, turn to the One who has *all* the answers; turn to the only One who loves you enough to share His wisdom and His plans with you.

> *"For I know the plans I have for you," declares the Lord, "plans for welfare and not for calamity to give you a future and a hope. Then you will call upon Me and come and pray to Me, and I will listen to you. You will seek Me and find Me when you search for Me with all your heart."* (Jer. 29:11–13)

> *Therefore, since we have a great high priest who has passed through the heavens, Jesus the Son of God, let us hold fast our confession. For we do not have a high priest who cannot sympathize with our weaknesses, but One who has been tempted in all things as we are, yet without sin. Therefore* ***let us draw near with confidence to the throne of grace, so that we may receive mercy and find grace to help in time of need.*** (Heb. 4:14–16; emphasis mine)

These verses tell us clearly that we have help available to us. More importantly, verse 16 tells us that the grace we need for our help is already there! It says we can *find grace.* You can't find something that's not there! If you can get to the place in your heart where you believe that our all-powerful Lord, the God of all creation was so touched by the human condition that it brought tears to His eyes, then you have embarked on a journey of overwhelming love and trust with God—the same journey that God intended to have with Adam and Eve, which I will address before this chapter ends. For now, you need only understand that God has already provided all the love and grace you will ever need. Your job is to acquire it. ***Your labor is not to convince God to do something He's already done*** (according to this passage) but to labor to accept it, claim it, possess it, and appropriate it! That, my friends, is what faith is all about.

We Have Disconnected Ourselves from the Source

The fact that people aren't sure that they are significant to God manifests itself in this one area regarding His role, presence, and involvement in our prayers. I speak with people every day who fully, unconditionally, and wholeheartedly believe in God. But if you ask them if they believe God will respond to their prayer requests and change things for the better, well, they're not as fully convinced about that. The area of biggest doubt for them lies with matters of health and healing (Mary and Martha will reinforce this for you when you read chapter 2).

One Big Flip-Flop

If we look back in history at the gospel of Mark when Jesus was teaching a throng in a crowded house, we see an event that has to make us wonder: "what happened?" and "what changed?" Mankind's flip-flop is monumental! Let's look at Mark 2:

> *When He had come back to Capernaum several days afterward it was heard that He was at home. And many were gathered together, so that there was no longer room, not even near the door; and He was speaking the word to them. And they came, bringing to Him a paralytic, carried by four men. Being unable to get to Him because of the crowd, they removed the roof above Him; and when they had dug an opening, they let down the pallet on which the paralytic was lying. And Jesus seeing their faith said to the paralytic,* ***"Son, your sins are forgiven."*** *But some of the scribes* (Scribes were

> members of the Pharisees' party. They were professional students, defenders of the law as judges in the Sanhedrin) *were sitting there and reasoning in their hearts, "Why does this man speak that way? He is blaspheming; who can forgive sins but God alone?" Immediately Jesus, aware in His spirit that they were reasoning that way within themselves, said to them,* ***"Why are you reasoning about these things in your hearts? Which is easier to say to the paralytic, 'Your sins are forgiven'; or to say, 'Get up, and pick up your pallet and walk'? But so that you may know that the Son of Man has authority on earth to forgive sins"****—He said to the paralytic,* ***"I say to you, get up, pick up your pallet and go home."*** *And he got up and immediately picked up the pallet and went out in the sight of everyone, so that they were all amazed and 'were glorifying God, saying, "We have never seen anything like this."* (Mark 2:1–12; emphasis mine)

Here's the flip-flop: everyone flocked to Jesus when He was preaching or visiting their towns because *they knew they could be healed*—even if they simply sat where His shadow would pass over them. The doubts about Jesus were about His ability to forgive their sins and grant them eternal life as the passage in Mark verifies. By Jewish belief, that was blasphemy.

What about today? If you have accepted Jesus Christ as your Lord and Savior, you have no doubt that your sins are forgiven by His finished work on the cross and that you will spend eternity in heaven. You have this thing called "paradise," "the hereafter," and "life after death" all wrapped up in a neat little package of theology that makes complete sense to you; but what about pre-paradise? What about your time here on earth? If, as promised, Jesus is giving you His peace and His joy, how does that reconcile with your broken, disease-filled body? Where's the peace and joy in that? Why do our prayers seem to go unanswered? Are we to be stoic and fatalistic and accept that our condition is simply "God's Will"? Really?

The silence between your asking and God's answering is deafening. I want to know "why?"— And so should you! How can you get to a point where you believe you will be healed of your sickness? Why are the four gospels filled with healings? What's ***that*** message all about if it no longer applies?

Does the physical absence of Christ cast doubt? Do we as a society need to see, feel, touch, or hear in order to believe?

Christ is now seated at the right hand of God in heaven. He has sent His Spirit the Comforter, to us. Christians accept those two facts. The problem is that "heaven" and "spirit" are abstract nouns; descriptions without shape or dimension. Just ask someone to describe what the Holy Spirit looks like. Our difficulty in claiming and accepting healing doesn't rely on God's *ability* to heal, just like it didn't in biblical times; it self-destructs because of the physical absence of the healer! But God in His wisdom knew this would be an issue. Look what He says in the book of John.

After Christ's resurrection, He appeared before the disciples but Thomas was absent. When told that the others had seen the Lord, Thomas expressed doubt, saying he would have to see and touch the holes the nails made in Christ's hands before he would believe. John 20:29 records this scene as Christ appeared again before Thomas and the others, "***Because you have seen Me have you believed? Blessed are they who did not see, and yet believed.***"

"We" are ***they***. We haven't seen our Lord, but Christ is clear; we will be blessed if we believe. Well, that's all well and good Pastor Clark, I *do believe* that Christ is the Son of God, but I have a hard time believing He will heal my heart disease, my diabetes, my cancer. My answer to that is simple. You don't fully understand just how much God cares for you. ***Until you can understand how much God loved Jesus, you won't understand how much He loves you***.

When Worth Met Value

Have you ever gone shopping and found that the price for the things you wanted to buy is just too high? Perhaps for the ladies, it is a nice pair of boots or a purse but those boots you like are $64.99. You were hoping for something around $45.00. And over there on the next aisle are some beautiful purses, but they are the same price as the boots. You decide that $130.00 to buy both items is just too much to pay. And for you guys, a silk tie is $31.00 and a nice shirt with French Cuffs to go with it is $62.00. So, what do we do? We go through this evaluation process of trying to decide if what we are willing to pay is worth the price or value requested. We do it with everything. If a steak and egg breakfast is listed at $12.00, we'll probably get the pancakes for $6.95. It's a constant back and forth: is the worth of what I'm about to acquire deserving of the value I'm about to give up? Is the worth, expressed in usefulness or importance a fair return for exchanging something I currently have, value and appreciate?

God faced this exchange decision. He made the choice that the value of His children's souls being with Him for eternity was worth the life of His Son, Jesus Christ. 'My Son for your soul'. 'My only begotten Son for your sin; your hatred, your lecherous and murderous hearts.'

Here's the irony: God paid the full price for all of mankind; but in the end only a small percentage accepted the exchange. Did God pay too much? No. Jesus saw your worth on the cross and willingly exchanged His Righteousness for your sin; willingly exchanged His wholesome body for your diseased and decaying body. This is how much God loves you and values you.

In Mozart's *Requiem*, there is a passage that illustrates Christ's love for us: Mozart, representing the human condition, writes, "*Remember Merciful Jesus that* ***I am the cause of Your journey***."

Prophesied Healing and Love

Let's travel back a little further in time to another scripture about healing. The author is the prophet Isaiah, writing around 700 BC. Chapter 53 is all about prophesying Christ's life and suffering. Look at Isaiah 53:4: "*Surely our griefs He Himself bore, and our sorrows He carried.*"

"Griefs" in the original Hebrew is the word ***choliy*** *(pronounced khol-ee).* Here are the meanings according to *The New Strong's Expanded Dictionary of Bible Words:* ***malady, anxiety, calamity, sickness, disease, grief, sick.*** *Strong's* goes on to say this: *Choliy means "sickness". The use of this word in the description of the Suffering Servant in Isaiah 53:3–4 is rendered "grief". The meaning of "sickness" occurs in Deuteronomy 7:15: "The Lord will remove from you all sickness; and He will not put on you any of the harmful diseases of Egypt which you have known."*

"Sorrows" in the Greek is ***odune*** *(pronounced od-oo-nay).* Once again, using *Strong's*, the translations are ***pain, consuming grief, distress.*** In relation to the heart, it describes ***great heaviness and continual sorrow.***

Let's use a little poetic license and rewrite Isaiah 53:4 because you really need to get this. Here we go: **Clark 53:4**, "*Surely our maladies, our anxieties, our calamities, our sicknesses, our diseases, our griefs* ***He himself bore****, and our pain and consuming grief, the great heaviness in our heart, the distress and nagging and unending sorrow in our hearts,* ***He carried.***"

Wow! And some of you are struggling with the fact that ***Jesus wept!*** These are some of the things Jesus did *after* He wept!

Have you ever watched any of those consumer commercials on television? They pitch this wonderful product and give you a price and then the announcer says, "But wait! There's more!" Well, that's exactly what Isaiah could have said. "But wait, there's more!" After telling us that all our diseases, infirmities, addictions, afflictions, griefs and sorrows have been put away at the cross (in other words, our healing has been secured), Isaiah 53:5, the very next verse, tells us what we have always cherished about our faith: "*But He was pierced through for our transgressions, He was crushed for our iniquities; the chastening for our well-being fell upon Him.*" This passage tells us our sins have been forgiven—borne by our Lord. He who knew no sin was found sinful, while we who did no right became righteous.

But don't lose sight of the fact that this passage comes ***after*** Isaiah tells us that Christ's journey to the cross has given us **access to a completely healthy and prosperous life!** This isn't a coincidence. First, Christ took care of our peace and joy on this earth by removing our ailments—all of them! Then, once our earthly life was over, He assured us that because of His righteousness, our sins would be forgiven, and we would spend eternity with Him in heaven. Are you starting to see how much we are loved?

When Jesus wept at the sorrow and sadness of the human condition in John 11:35, He showed the world not only His compassion but also how our lack of faith grieves Him. We pray to a God who not only understands what our concerns are; a God who has endured everything we could possibly experience, but according to this verse, He cares so much that it brings Him to tears! There's simply no reason for you to not expect to be healed. Healing has *already happened—on the cross!* Your only job is to claim it, not pray for it, but claim His finished work. **Another way of saying this is that faith is the acquisition, the acceptance, the appropriation of grace in its many manifestations**.

There's a story about Commander Alan Shepard, an astronaut in the early days of America's space program. He flew the Mercury capsule, Freedom 7, and was the first American to launch into space. When asked what he was thinking about while sitting atop the Redstone rocket that would send him into new frontiers, Shepard replied, "*That every part of this rocket was put together by the lowest bidder!*"

Dear friends, let me assure you that your journey through the remainder of this life and on into the next was orchestrated and put together by the ***highest bidder! Jesus Christ!***

Why then do so many of us feel that God is too busy, too preoccupied, too otherwise engaged, too Holy to give insignificant ones such as us an audience. Why would a mighty God stoop to my level?

The intent of this book is to first ***teach you that your prayers mean something to God because of who you are;*** and second, ***teach you about manifesting your urgent requests because of who God is***. Before we go any further, I want you to "camp" on a few definitions of prayer, add some of your own and then take ownership of the ones that are the most appealing to you.

- Prayer gives you a voice in eternity.
- Prayer gives you a role in deliverance.
- Prayer allows you to discover *who you are* and acknowledge *who God is.*
- Prayer allows you to *fast spiritually.* When you let go and let God, the secular part of you that wants control departs allowing the divinity of God to enter and lead.
- Prayer allows you to worship and glorify your Creator.
- Prayer restores you to the garden of peace, harmony, and coexistence. We were created to live in a garden, but we spend our lives as if we're in the middle of a freeway.
- Prayer enters into and has an effect on the spirit world.
- Prayer gives you an opportunity to feel His Holiness.

Who Are We?

Before we look at the final thoughts for this chapter, I want to spend a few minutes examining who we are. Many of us allow the world to define us. We can either be elevated in status by our adoring public, or we can be shot down in flames by people who don't adore us. The expression "keeping up with the Joneses" actually means something in our society. Even in church circles, pastors use attendance numbers to define their church, their success; and I suppose, way down deep, their prowess in the pulpit.

In general, we are influenced the most by our environment. For example, if you live in the Bronx, you don't want to walk around the neighborhood sporting a Red Sox jersey. If you are going to Ohio State University, don't wear a Michigan hat to class.

As adults, we struggle with worldly and family expectations. Things like how we dress, how we act, how successful we are, or what kind of car we drive. In some families, not being married is a stigma.

As youths, we struggle to be popular, to run with the "in crowd". Brighter students may intentionally "dumb down" in order to be accepted by a certain element. Young people may feel the need to be sexually active in order to fit in, or to try drugs to be "cool".

These influences don't only come from the home or from church; most of them come from the world. They come from the pressure to be accepted; to have worth; or in some cases, to be in control. At this age, bullies can change lives. What I am going to share with you in a few minutes will assure you of the worth God gave you.

A few years ago, psychologist Ruth W. Berenda and her associates carried out an interesting experiment with teenagers designed to show how a person handled group pressure. The plan was simple. They brought groups of ten adolescents into a room for a test. Subsequently, each group of ten was instructed to raise their hands when the teacher pointed to the longest line on three separate charts. What one person in the group did not know was that nine of the others in the room had been instructed ahead of time to vote for the *second longest line!*

Regardless of the instructions they heard, once they were all together in the group, the nine were not to vote for the longest line but rather vote for the second longest line. The experiment began with nine teenagers voting for the wrong line. The stooge would typically glance around, frown in confusion, and slip his hand up with the group. The instructions were repeated and thc next card was raised. Time after time, the self-conscious stooge would sit there saying a short line was longer than a long line, simply because he lacked the courage to challenge the group. This remarkable conformity occurred in about 75 percent of the cases, and was true of small children and high school students as well.[2]

Geographical influences are natural and understandable. When social and moral influences change who you are, then those are much bigger and more dangerous issues. There's truth in the expression "If you don't stand for anything, you'll fall for everything." So let's look at who we were meant to be and what we can stand on.

How Did God Create You with Worth?

The first human ever to walk the earth was named Adam. The Hebrew word for Adam is ***Adam*** and literally means "man, mankind or people". In every sense, each of these translations is plural and can be extended to include you and me. God's actions regarding Adam apply equally to us when we were created in our mothers' womb. It's interesting that the Hebrew word for earth is ***adamah***. *"Then the Lord God formed man of dust from the ground, and breathed into his nostrils the breath of life; and man became a living being"* (Gen. 2:7).

The Hebrew that is used for the word formed is ***yatsar*** (pronounced yaw-tsar). *Strong's* says it means "to mold into a form or shape as a potter". Other passages where the word is used are Isaiah 45:7, which says, "*I* ***form*** *the light and create darkness*"; Psalm 74:17, "*Thou* ***has made*** *summer and winter*"; Zechariah 12:1, "*God* ***formed*** *the spirit of man*"; as well as Psalm 33:15, "*He who* ***fashions*** *the hearts of them all.*"

Adam was molded or shaped from ***Adamah***. Well, that's interesting you say, but just linguistics. Yet, we have to wonder why man was formed from the lowliest part of Creation. We weren't formed from massive oak trees or giant sequoias; not from the towering mountains or puffy, majestic clouds or roaring oceans. Nope—just dust. The kind of stuff you kick up with your sneakers, or the annoying choking clouds that tractors throw into the sky when the farmer is tilling his land. Dust!

The redeeming feature is this nugget that I found on the website Aish.com:

> *The earth is a realm in which we can plant and yield fruits, giving rise to* ***new*** *life which was not there beforehand. Man's kinship with the ground, therefore, hints to his* ***greatest potential.*** *The met-*

> *aphor of the ground and its centrality in man's name is no coincidence. The simple act of planting a seed is a powerful symbol of man's potential. There is a very physical side to every human, and often that side of us brings us to places of rot and decay, places in which we can wreak more havoc on creation than the most destructive animal. Yet we also have the ability to transcend that downward pull and grow from the earth into something greater with almost unlimited potential'* (Emphasis added).

His Plan for You and Me

We find God's intentions for man in Genesis 1:

> *Then God said, "Let us make man in Our **image**, according to Our **likeness**; and let them **rule** over the fish of the sea and over the birds of the sky and over the cattle and over all the earth, and over every creeping thing that creeps on the earth."* (Gen. 1:26; emphasis mine)

Let's take this apart and unpack some of these words. The English language can be a little lazy or cavalier at times with translations, so here are the original thoughts in the original Hebrew language.

The word for *image* is ***tselem*** (pronounced tseh-lem), which involves several concepts such as ***a shadow, a phantom, a resemblance or an illusion***; *hence a representative figure.* The word means image in the sense of essential nature, i.e., human nature in its internal and external characteristics rather than an exact duplicate (of God). An illusion is something that tricks your senses. You've all seen "mirages" on the roadway ahead of you. It looks like there is water across the highway, but of course there isn't.

Then, back to Genesis 1:27, Adam, created in the image of God, would carry all the recognition and influence of God. Psalm 8 says that we were created just a little lower than God (New American standard).

Again, from Genesis 1:26, "*According to our* ***likeness.***" The Hebrew word is ***d'muwth*** (pronounced dem-ooth) and means "the original after which a thing is patterned."

We see then, that God *patterned* Adam (and by extension, us), according to the original being, God Himself; so that he was as closely similar to God as would be a *shadow, a phantom or an illusion,* having all the *recognition and influence* of God..

God, in all His creativity and imagination, created all the multitudes of flora (trees, plants, crops) of different appearance, color, size, shape, and function. After that, He created the thousands of species of fish and crustaceans that fill our lakes, rivers, and oceans (the Bible calls them swarms of living creatures); then He filled the heavens with flying things of all sizes and descriptions, and then He filled the earth with all kinds of different looking, different functioning animals. Just look around at the incredible imagination that God used to create these things.

Why then did God suddenly appear to abandon His creativity when He created us? The Bible tells us we are created in "*His image, according to His likeness.*" No other creature or plant is created in His image or likeness. Can this possibly be the beginning of an understanding that God actually planned to have a partnership with those who so closely resemble Him? God, working hand in hand with mankind who, because of his similarity to God, would garner all the same respect, reverence, and authority as would God Himself! Can you find any similar partnership in any sense of the word between God and the rest of creation?

Man has dominion over all other aspects of God's creation ("*And let them* ***rule*** *over the fish of the sea and over the birds of the sky and over the cattle and over all the earth, and over every creeping thing that creeps on the earth.*")

The Hebrew word for *rule* is ***mashal*** (pronounced maw-shal) and means "to rule, reign or have dominion". One has to wonder if

God wanted man to so resemble Himself that when he (man) was regarded by other creatures, they would see God in him. God created a hierarchy whereby man has dominion over earth's creatures and physical features, and God has dominion over man. In this partnership with God, man assists God in getting His plans done on earth. In fact, man is so similar to God and resembles God to such an extent that it's not a stretch to think of man as God's *representative.* One name we *can* ascribe to early man is that he was God's *intercessor*; the one who interceded between God's creation and God. As God's *representative* or *intercessor*, Adam became God's mediator.

So what does it really mean to **represent** someone? The dictionary defines it as "present again". Perhaps we can say it like this: an attorney for example re-*presents* the actions of his client to the judge. A teacher re-*presents* the text books that someone else has written. A pastor re-*presents* the word of God. But look at these other meanings the dictionary gives: "*to exhibit the image and counterpart of; to speak and act with authority on the part of; to be a substitute or agent for.*"[3]

Then man (you and I included) would be expected to re-*present* God's will on earth. First Corinthians 11:7 tells us that "*man is the image and glory of God.*" God needs to be recognized in humanity so that we can accurately represent Him![4]

I wonder if God is still recognized in human kind. When you look at the crowd in a football stadium, do you see God? How about when you line up at McDonald's for your burger, do you see God in the people in line or seated? When you see violence on television, little league fathers getting into it, do you see God? Does mankind, in whatever scenario, remind you of God? Our lifelong struggle and God's deepest desire is that we change back into God's image "*from glory to glory*" (2 Cor. 3:18).

Let's summarize because we've taken on a lot in the last page or so:

1. Adam (and us) was created so similar to God that he (us) gave the appearance of an illusion, a phantom, and a shadow (of God).
2. Because of the illusion, God was seen in Adam, which meant that Adam had all authority on earth and carried the weight of the Almighty.

3. Adam spoke and acted with the authority of God presenting (representing) the will of God on earth.
4. Adam was God's governor or manager here.
5. Earth was under Adam's care. He was the watchman or guardian! It was his assignment.[5]

In wrapping your mind around all of this, the authorities and responsibilities that God gave to Adam and the expectations God had for His children didn't then, and doesn't now mean that God abdicated His creation to man. What it means is that God has invested heavily through all of this to structure a ***partnership covenant*** with His creation. Because God loves His children so much, He trusts us to work with Him to accomplish His will on earth for His people. We get to play a role in the deliverance of God's creation!

God's first intercessor, Adam, was without sin until he and Eve ate of the tree of the knowledge of good and evil. The sin nature from that disobedience is with you and me to this day. But let's be clear—sin is *not* genetic! Scientists will never find a sin gene! God's second intercessor, His Son Jesus, was also without sin but instead of giving away the authority given to Him, Jesus has begun to reclaim the territory given to Satan by Adam. We are part of that reclamation. We are still in the partnership equation. After the first intercessor fell, man was deemed sinful and God placed him under a set of laws. After the Second Intercessor prevailed, believers were deemed righteous and placed under grace.

God Cherishes Your Prayers

We have so much sin in our world because we crave it. God continually seeks people willing to work with Him to bring about change. First Chronicles 28 sums up God's search and man's reward:

> *As for you, my son Solomon, know the God of your father, and serve Him with a whole heart and a willing mind; for the Lord searches all hearts, and*

> *understands every intent of the thoughts. If you seek Him, He will let you find Him; but if you forsake Him, He will reject you forever.* (1 Chron. 28:9)

There are two sides to prayer; yours which is to fellowship with God with your whole heart and willing mind so that you can understand how God's assignment will work in your life. The other side is God's side; He cherishes your prayers and the fellowship because He has assignments for us:

- He needs us to step up in faith and stand in the gap.
- He needs people to step out and speak up as new modern-day prophets.
- God needs leaders to reel in corruption and promote His glory instead of Satan's depravity.
- He needs humans to go on missions, to evangelize, to lay hands on the sick, and to raise up the weak.

Your prayers don't go unheard, don't end up on a to-do list, aren't inconsequential. Your prayer life means everything to God. After everything He's been through with us humans, He welcomes your fellowship, your partnership. His greatest desire is to restore your joy—your peaceful earthly existence. He's waiting to embrace your return. We are all "prodigal sons," and the results are the same every time we turn to God and pray. He's waiting to welcome us home. In this respect, it *is* "**all about us**."

A Project for You

The next time you go to prayer, acknowledge that God created you as similar to Himself as possible so that you would be equipped to carry out His assignment for your life. Ask God to reveal to you what that assignment is, and that He would give you the wisdom and resources to carry it out.

2

Jesus Wept

Billy Graham once said, "Heaven is full of prayers that have never been asked." Many of the people I have talked to might tweak that statement to, "Heaven is full of prayers that have never been answered."

There's absolutely no way to prove this, but I'm thinking that, at some point, ***every single person who has ever prayed to God*** since Noah and the great flood has asked these two questions: "where are You, God?" and "why have you not answered my prayer?" I'm in that group, and I think you probably are too. In fact, the more desperate your prayers, the more possibility that you have wondered, *God, where are you in my time of need?*

If that silence between you and God bothers you, let me offer you some comfort by telling you that Christ is also in our group. Matthew 27:46 reveals Christ's pain on the cross when He uttered: "*My God, My God, Why have You forsaken Me?*"

So Many Possible Reasons, but One Thing Stands Out

Future chapters will help you understand some additional factors that impact *how* you pray. Things like God's timing, God's will and our persistence. And did you know that your prayers can be hijacked? We'll look at the severity of your circumstances—are some things just too small to bother God with? What about our prayers for others? Does God pay attention to our intercessions? And what are Prayer Bowls all about? We'll get into all of them, but let's start with this: *the most important factor in your prayer life is* ***FAITH!***

Why *Did* Jesus Weep?

Is there a connection between "unanswered" prayer and faith; between faith and Jesus weeping; between Jesus weeping and "unanswered" prayer? The short answer is yes, and it's profound.

So let's get right to the point; **why *did* Jesus weep—twice?** (Luke 19:41–44 and John 11:35) and how does His weeping *help* your prayer life? Listen carefully—**the weeping is a warning, an alert, a heads-up**. Let me wade into this with an allegory:

> *A very wealthy individual had the resources to give generously without any appreciable impact on his prosperity. He had helped many individuals in his family but the one who needed his help the most, his daughter, wanted nothing to do with his help or his lifestyle.*
>
> *She had shunned the idea of going to college, preferring instead to hang with her friends on the street, writing her poetry and playing her guitar. Everyone in her group panhandled to make a few bucks so they could enjoy their subsistence living and smoke a joint together every now and then. As winter approached with its freezing temperatures, the father, worried for his daughter's well-being, went*

out and found her one evening, shivering, cold, hungry and exhausted from lack of sleep.

Embarrassed in front of her 'friends', she wanted nothing to do with his offer of help. She preferred her independence, 'knowing' that listening to her father would require some changes to her life. She just 'knew' that accepting his help would bring all kinds of demands with it; 'do this', 'do that'; 'obey me or I'll cut you off'. She could just see it. She dismissed him with a wave of her hand and turned away, toward her friend. None of her fears could be allayed, and dad brushed a tear from his cheek as he left without her.

He had tried to assure her that, as his child, he only cared about her well-being; that the only string attached to his offer of help was for her to simply accept it.

Before that winter ended, her dehydrated, hypothermic, lifeless body was found in an alley, huddled for warmth next to her friends. Again, this time at her funeral, dad wept uncontrollably. If only she had listened to him.

Two Warnings

The story of Jesus weeping in the Lazarus context (the one we will study in greater detail in this chapter) has gained a lot of attention in Christian circles. People will tell you it's the shortest verse in the Bible. Well, sorry—it isn't: First Thessalonians 5:16 says, "*Rejoice always.*" So really, it's tied for the shortest verse in the Bible! Perhaps the verse has notoriety because we don't expect to see God cry; just like we don't like to see our superheroes from Hollywood defeated. But God did cry—***twice***; in fact, within a few days of each other.

Let's look at the second (chronologically) warning first because it shows graphically, the consequences of unbelief; the foreshadowing of the hell awaiting nonbelievers.

The Second Warning—Jerusalem

On the Sunday before His crucifixion (we refer to it as Palm Sunday), Jesus was approaching Jerusalem where he would be welcomed as a hero, only to be betrayed before the week ended. He wept as he came to a hill overlooking the city. Let's read the full account in Luke 19:

> *When He approached Jerusalem, He saw the city and* ***wept over it****, saying, "****If you had known in this day, even you, the things which make for peace! But now they have been hidden from your eyes. For the days will come upon you when your enemies will throw up a barricade against you and surround you and hem you in on every side, and they will level you to the ground and your children within you, and they will not leave in you one stone upon another, because you did not recognize the time of your visitation.****"* (Luke 19:41–44; emphasis mine)

The Jews thought that Christ was going to be their earthly king and overturn the oppression they faced under the Roman occupation. When they realized this was not going to happen, they and their leaders turned on Him and crucified Him—just five days later.

Christ's warning in Luke became a reality approximately thirty-five to forty years after His death as Jerusalem and the temple were destroyed by the Romans. Allow me to introduce the man who gave us such a brutal and gory account of the events.

Flavius Josephus, also known as Joseph Ben Matthias (Yosef Ben Mattityahu), was born to a priestly Jewish family just five or so years after Christ was crucified. When Josephus was young, he was a diplomat in Rome and eventually led Jewish forces against Rome. After he was captured, Josephus escaped imprisonment by willingly serving Roman authorities, acting as an interpreter for the Romans during the war. Afterward, he lived in Rome and wrote books about the war and the history of the Jews.

Listen to how Josephus describes the destruction of Jerusalem:

> *All hope of escape and all food supplies were cut off from the Jews. Famine devoured thousands upon thousands. The alleys were choked with bodies. The survivors were too weak to bury the dead. Some fell into graves with them. No mourning was heard in Jerusalem, for famine stifled all emotions, and an awful silence shrouded the city.*
>
> *One refugee who had been in charge of a single gate, told the [Roman General] that [nearly 16,000] corpses had been carried out in an 11-week period. Other leaders reported 600,000 bodies of the lower classes had been thrown out, and it was impossible to number the rest.*

Other scholars have estimated that 1.1 million Jews were killed by the Roman armies and over a hundred thousand were enslaved.

Had they listened to Christ, would Jerusalem have been spared? Would the Roman Empire still march through Western Europe and into England before its eventual demise? We have most of the Old Testament to assure us that God would have brought victory to Israel over the Romans because He had helped them defeat countless enemies since their exodus from Egypt. As for the fate of the Roman Empire, we simply have no way to know. What we *do* know is that Josephus's writings and Christ's predictions are eerily congruent.

A Lesson for You and Me

Christ weeping at the impending loss of salvation puts emotion into something He said in Matthew 18:14, "*So it is not the will of your Father who is in heaven that one of these little ones perish.*" He gives us a choice and choices have consequences. But it broke His heart.

The Covenant He offers us is simple: *Believe in My Son and I will give you eternal life.* I have to wonder if Christ continues to weep today when He himself speculated in Luke 18:8, "*However, when the son of man comes* [returns] *will He find faith on the earth?*"

Jerusalem's destruction along with such a massive loss of life is not just a mere history lesson. It's a lesson to all generations who are deciding to turn *to* God or turn *from* God. The consequences are predictable.

God, asking His people to turn back to Him, says this in Deuteronomy 30, "*If you turn to the Lord your God with all your heart and soul... for this commandment which I command you today* ***is not too difficult for you, nor is it out of reach***" (Deut. 30:10–11; emphasis mine).

And here are the consequences, found a few verses later in verse 19, "*I call heaven and earth to witness against you today, that I have set before you life and death, the blessing and the curse. So choose life in order that you may live, you and your descendants.*"

Jerusalem chose death. Christ wept, knowing she had chosen poorly despite His three years of ministry. He even admonished them; to no avail:

> *O Jerusalem, Jerusalem, the city that kills the prophets and stones those sent to her! How often I wanted to gather your children together, just as a hen gathers her brood under her wings, and you would not have it! Behold, your house is left to you desolate; and I say to you, you will not see Me until the time comes when you say, "Blessed is He who comes in the name of the Lord!"* (Luke 13:34–35)

Jerusalem and all of Judea had witnessed or heard about Christ's miracles and teachings. The witnessing produced a quasi-faith in Him. They believed what He had done and what He could do; but they didn't believe He was the Son of God, able to give them salvation.

Where are we? By accepting Christ as God's Son, we seal our salvation and eternal life. But do we have enough faith to trust the rest of the New Covenant? Do we carry guilt from our sins? Do we worry about medical diagnoses? Are we simply unable to give our addictions to God and walk away, whole? Have we, unwittingly, cherry-picked the New Covenant and as a result live troubled, less-than-joyful lives?

Are we so immersed in our own selves, our lifestyles, our friends and acquaintances, our jobs, our plans for a new car or house, etc., etc., etc., that some or all of Christ's prophesies in Matthew will prevail over our tenuous faith? What happens if we turn away from our faith because life becomes so difficult? Let's take a look at Christ's end-time remarks.

> *You will be hearing of wars and rumors of wars. See that you are not frightened, for those things must take place, but that is not yet the end. For nation will rise against nation, and kingdom against kingdom, and in various places there will be famines and earthquakes. But all these things are merely the beginning of birth pangs. Then they will deliver you to tribulation, and will kill you, and you will be hated by all nations because of My name. At that time many will fall away and will betray one another and hate one another. Many false prophets will arise and will mislead many. Because lawlessness is increased, most people's love will grow cold. But the one who endures to the end, he will be saved.* (Matt. 24:6–13)

Christ's warnings to us continue for another thirty-eight verses. Please read them when you get a chance. These are the concerns that

Jesus worries about in the Luke 18:8 passage above. Will He find faith when He returns?

Be honest for a minute. How long do you spend in prayer each day? Do you ever just have conversations with God? Do you spend time in His Word? In other words, do you know Him well enough to preserve your faith when these Matthew 24 moments arise in your life?

Your prayers, your conversations, your praises all deliver you directly into the existence and authority of your Creator. The Jews did not recognize the impact of their time with Him. If we allow Him to diminish in our lives because we aren't getting immediate answers to prayers, our hard-heartedness will begin to look like that of Israel's. When that happens, millions more will not hear the Gospel story because we won't have the enthusiasm to deliver it.

The First Warning—Lazarus

The first time Jesus wept (the Lazarus story) is quite similar both in reason and in results. He saw that people, *even His very closest friends*, hadn't understood His message—His message of salvation.

Let's go back to the beginning of the chapter:

> *Now a certain man was sick, Lazarus of Bethany, the village of Mary and her sister Martha. It was the Mary who anointed the Lord with ointment, and wiped His feet with her hair, whose brother Lazarus was sick. So the sisters sent word to Him, saying, "Lord, behold, he whom You love is sick." But when Jesus heard this, He said, "**this sickness is not to end in death, but for the glory of God, so that the Son of God may be glorified by it.**"* (John 11:1–4; emphasis mine)

First of all, I believe that the Bible is absolute truth. I believe that every word, every phrase is in the right place at the right time for the full revelation of our Mighty God.

Verses 1 and 2 above state that Lazarus is sick ***before*** verse 3 tells us that the sisters sent word to Christ. I believe that Christ *knew* Lazarus was sick before he heard from the sisters! Let's read on and I will explain.

Verse 6 says, "*So when He heard that he was sick, He then stayed two days longer in the place where He was. Then after this He said to the disciples, 'Let us go to Judea again.*'" Verses 7–13 all take place as Christ and the disciples are preparing to leave for Judea and the city of Bethany.

In verse 11, while still in the place where they had received word of Lazarus's illness, Christ tells the disciples that Lazarus has fallen asleep and He needs to go to Bethany to waken him. The disciples ask the obvious question that if he is sleeping he'll awake by himself. Then in verse 14, Jesus says, "*Lazarus is dead.*" How did He know that? He said it twice—in verse 11 and in 14. There wasn't any further correspondence from Mary and Martha telling Him that. So if Christ knew Lazarus was dead, I believe He knew when he became sick. I'll show you later why this is important.

Verse 17 says, "*So when Jesus came* (to Bethany), *He found that He had already been in the tomb four days.*"

"**In the tomb four days**." The timing is important so let's dig a little deeper. After delaying two days and upon setting out for Judea, Christ announces to the disciples that Lazarus is dead (v. 14). When Jesus arrived in Judea, He learns that Lazarus has been dead for four days (v. 17). Then it must have taken Christ and His disciples four days to travel to Judea! If we assume that the word Martha and Mary sent to Christ also took four days to get to Him (same journey, same distance—only in reverse), then ten days (including the two days He delayed) passed between the time the sisters sent word and Christ actually arrived in Judea!

So to recap, we've assumed that Christ knew when Lazarus became sick, simply because He knew without any further word that he was dead. Jesus delayed two days; He then took four days to get to Bethany, which implies that the sisters' letter took four days to reach Jesus. Total—ten days.

Let's look at some geography to convince you that ten days passed since the sisters wrote to Jesus telling Him that Lazarus was sick.

The previous chapter, John 10:22–23, tells us that Christ is in Jerusalem for the Feast of the Dedication. The next several verses tell us He was teaching in the temple and the Jews, incensed at His words, were ready to stone Him (v. 31). Verses 39–40 will put the geography in place for you, "*Therefore they were seeking again to seize Him, and He eluded their grasp. And He went away again beyond the Jordan to the place where John was first baptizing, and He was staying there.*"

Where was John the Baptist ***first*** baptizing? John 1:28 says, "*These things took place in* ***Bethany beyond the Jordan****, where John was baptizing*" (emphasis added).

This is not the Bethany where Lazarus and his sisters lived. Biblical scholars call this place Bethabara. It is located "beyond the Jordan" or east of the Jordan River, about ten miles south of the Sea of Galilee and approximately forty miles north and east of Jerusalem (where Jesus was about to be stoned).

Verse 7 above tells us that Jesus said, "*Let us go to Judea again.*" Bethany, His destination, is in Judea; Bethabara is not. It's part of a ten city region called Decapolis. Five of the cities are immediately east of the Sea of Galilee. The northern most city is Damascus, Syria which is about 136 miles from Jerusalem. It's not beyond reason that a forty-mile journey would take four days.

So why is all of this important? Verses 21 and 32 both tell us that the sisters take turns telling Jesus that if He had been there, Lazarus would not have died. Those two statements by the sisters exhibit a lot of faith in Christ. It was like they said, "*Look, I have believed in You; I have seen the miracles You have performed; the sicknesses You have healed. I just know in my heart that if You had been here (come right away), Lazarus would still be alive.*"

Now, here's the crux of the entire passage: In verses 25 and 26, Jesus tells Martha, "*I am the resurrection and the life; he who believes in Me will live even if he dies. And everyone who lives and believes in Me will never die. Do you believe this?*"

Martha responds in verse 27, "*Yes, Lord; I have believed that You are the Christ, the Son of God, even He that comes into the world.*"

Wow! Those are the very same words that you and I say or have said at least once in our lives. Haven't we? Christ tells Martha that He is the resurrection and the life—that believers will live even if they die, and Martha says, "I know! I know! I believe You!"

But later in the story, Jesus sees Mary (and presumably Martha) weeping as well as other mourners (v. 33–35) and "*He was deeply moved in spirit and was troubled, and said,* ***'Where have you laid him?'*** *They said to Him, Lord, come and see. Jesus wept.*"

Now there has been some speculation as to why Jesus wept. Some have said He wept because His friend Lazarus was dead; some have claimed that His compassion was awakened seeing so many family and friends weeping.

Here's what catches my eye: Verse 33 says, "*He was deeply moved in spirit...*" (That could apply to the compassion claims); but the verse continues with "*and was troubled.*" ***Troubled!*** Why? What would trouble Christ about seeing everyone weeping, knowing full well that He intended to raise Lazarus from the tomb?

Consider this: Christ is rapidly approaching the end of His ministry. Very soon, He will triumphantly enter into Jerusalem for Passover but in that week, He will face His arrest and crucifixion. His ministry is nearly over. After three years of teaching and healing and manifesting miraculous signs, Christ sees that despite followers' proclamations that He is the Son of God, the Christ, the Messiah, the one spoken of in Jewish prophecy, He witnesses His closest friends, the ones who know Him best, weeping over death. Even Mary and Martha are weeping their good-byes to Lazarus! (Revisit verse 27).

I believe Christ is weeping because despite His ministry, despite His journey which will take Him to the cross, people still don't get it (the same reason He wept over Jerusalem, above). He weeps because the faith they need for healing, for resurrecting life, for victory is verbalized but not internalized. I believe that Christ weeps today because you and I believe exactly as Martha believed; but when your family member is lying in that hospital, near death; when your home is days from foreclosure; when your son or daughter is losing the battle with addiction, we weep our good-byes; our faith falls short; and Christ weeps *again* because our faith is so frail.

If we can just understand that Christ is saying, "*It breaks My heart that you don't trust Me. What more can I do? I can't love you any more than I do. I've travelled nine hundred and ninety nine of the thousand steps to meet your needs; please take the last one to claim them.*"

Before we leave this passage, look with me at verses 38–40: "*So Jesus, again being deeply moved within, came to the tomb. Now it was a cave, and a stone was lying against it. Jesus said* ***'Remove the stone.'*** *Martha, the sister of the deceased, said to Him, 'Lord, by this time there will be a stench, for he has been dead four days.' Jesus said to her,* ***'Did I not say to you that if you believe, you will see the glory of God?'***" (emphasis added).

I want to look at 2 Peter 1:3: "*Seeing that His divine power has granted to us everything pertaining to life and godliness, through the true knowledge of Him who called us by His own glory and excellence.*"

A synonym for ***divine power*** is **Grace**. So I might say of this passage in 2 Peter, "*God's glory and excellence, providing amazing grace, gives us everything we need for life and holiness.*"

Applying this thought to John 11:40, we might say, "*By faith, you will see the glory and excellence of God providing the grace that brings life and holiness.*"

God's grace or divine power has provided everything you and I need for life and godliness or holiness. This divine power has already overcome (at the cross), death, sin, disease, poverty, addiction, relational issues, and everything else that might attack your life. Our job is to appropriate it, to take hold of it, to internalize it.

Well, Pastor Clark, I've been praying for years that God would heal my back, and it's just as bad now as it was back then. And therein lies your problem. You've been praying that God would do something that He has already done! You have turned a spiritual event (prayer) into a labor of works. You have effectively moved out from under the grace of 2 Peter 1:3 and now operate under the law that Romans 8:2 tells us brings death.

When you have more faith and more confidence in what you have done or are doing than what Jesus has already done, then you fall out of grace and into law! Remember this: under the law that was given to Moses, God says over and over, "Thou shalt not…, thou shalt not…, thou shalt not…" But under grace, God says, "I will…, I will…, I will."

What happened in the ten days that elapsed from the time Christ knew of Lazarus's sickness until He actually arrived in Bethany? Did the family's faith get stronger? Perhaps it did up until the time Lazarus died. You can almost hear Mary and Martha consoling one another, "*It's okay, our Lord will be here any day now.*" As Lazarus got sicker and weaker, the conversation might have sounded like this, "*I guess our Lord isn't coming; He probably didn't get our message; it wasn't our Lord's will to save him; he's so sick now, we should prepare for his death. Let's call the rest of the family.*" In other words, their faith fell apart. We know that because they both told Christ that Lazarus would have lived if He had been there. What about us? Don't we react the same way? How long do you continue in prayer without answer before you say, "*I guess it's not God's will…*"

Christ uses the most extreme example of delay, He decides to stay where He is for a couple of days even though He knows how serious things are. He knows when Lazarus's condition begins to deteriorate. He even knows when he dies! Why would a loving God do that? Why would he put so many people through all that agony, worry, and heartbreak? Why does He do the same thing to us? Look again at John 11, "**But** *when Jesus heard (that Lazarus was sick), He said,* ***'this sickness is not to end in death, but for the glory of God, so that the Son of God may be glorified by it'***" (John 11:4; emphasis mine).

Once again, our job is to accept, appropriate, and/or acquire the provisions already granted through God's grace; and by doing that, we find peace and God is glorified. We need to remember that God knows every stage of our condition, just as He did with Lazarus. Sometimes, answers to prayer are delayed in order to bring other issues, events, and people into the equation so that God's victory will be full and for His glory. We will look very closely at this in subsequent chapters. But as we will see later in chapter 3, there are other reasons for delayed answers to prayer.

Something to Think About:

You may be in that in-between-time waiting for God to answer your prayers. Ten days may be too long for you to wait, or perhaps it's been months or years and you have grown weary. He is aware of your need; He knew it before you did, and He will take care of you.

Psalm 91:11 reads, "For He will give His angels charge concerning you, to guard you in all your ways."

3

Powers, Principalities, and the Evil Your Prayers Release!

Sinister title, don't you think? Well, this is a book about prayer, and I want you to know all aspects because they will help you understand when God is silent; when there are no answers and why you should not give up. It may be helpful to know what we are up against when we go into prayer. The Old Testament doesn't have a lot to say about evil or demonic forces. Of course, we learn early on in Genesis 3:4–5 about Satan's temptations, but most Old Testament references to evil spirits relate to pagan customs and idol worship.

There is one glaring exception, however, in the book of Daniel where God seems to allow us to glimpse beyond the realities we are so comfortable with in our earthly life and look into the abstract spiritual realm. Here we find an unusual, paranormal activity revealing demonic forces in the heavenlies.

Even Praying about One of God's Promises Can Take Time

The background to the story is that the Israelites were allowed by God to be taken into captivity in the year 605 BC by the future King Nebuchadnezzar of the Babylonian Empire because of Israel's idolatry and failure to keep the sabbatical year for the land. Their captivity in Babylon, based on God's promise in Jeremiah 25:11, was to last seventy years. Daniel takes it upon himself with a lengthy prayer in which he pleads for God to restore Jerusalem and its temple.

Before we get into the "evil in the heavenlies," I want you to look with me at Daniel 9:18. This passage is a perfect example of how to pray. Answered prayer comes from God's goodness, not our efforts to move Him to do something He has already done! "*O my God, incline Your ear and hear! Open Your eyes and see our desolations and the city which is called by Your name;* ***for we are not presenting our supplications before You on account of any merits of our own, but on account of Your great compassion***" (emphasis added). Some translations replace the phrase, "of any merits of our own" with the word "righteousness". Either way, Daniel is saying that it's not according to his efforts and works that he is petitioning God; rather he can petition God because of God's mercy, God's provision, God's compassion. I hope you don't miss this important doctrine.

Okay, on to the evil our prayers release. As I mentioned earlier, Daniel has been praying for the restoration of the temple and of Jerusalem and that God would allow the Israelites to return to Israel.

Let's look at Daniel 10:2: "*In those days, I Daniel, had been mourning (praying) for three entire weeks.*" After three entire weeks, did he get discouraged? No, doesn't seem like he did. Did he quit, assuming that God was not going to answer, or that it mustn't be God's will? No, we're not told anything about that. Did he get angry with God? Nope! He just continued to pray.

"*I did not eat any tasty food, nor did meat or wine enter my mouth, nor did I use any ointment (lotion, body fragrances, symbolic of rejoicing) at all until the entire three weeks were completed*" (Dan. 10:3). This issue was so important to Daniel that he entered into a partial fast for the entire period he was praying.

"*On the twenty-fourth day of the first month, while I was by the bank of the great river, that is, the Tigris, I lifted my eyes and looked and behold, there was a certain man dressed in linen, whose waist was girded with a belt of pure gold of Uphaz* (a famous gold region)" (Dan. 10:4–5). Daniel goes on to describe that the appearance of this "vision", who is an unnamed angel, completely rendered him without strength and drained his face of blood. He goes on to say that he was driven to his hands and knees trembling by the forceful persona of this heavenly being.

Watch Carefully

> *He said to me, "O Daniel, man of high esteem, understand the words that I am about to tell you and stand upright, for I have now been sent to you." And when he had spoken this word to me, I stood up trembling. Then he said to me, "Do not be afraid, Daniel, for* ***from the first day*** *that you set your heart on understanding this and on humbling yourself before your God,* ***your words were heard,*** *and I have come in response to your words.* ***But the prince of the kingdom of Persia was withstanding me for twenty-one days;*** *then behold, Michael, one of the chief princes, came to help me, for I had been left there with the kings of Persia."* (Dan. 10:11–13; emphasis mine)

Let's unpack this and try to get a grip on what is happening here and what continues to happen in our lives. Now it is known in these days that King Cyrus of Persia is favorably disposed toward the Jews; however, physical and spiritual powers hostile to the restoration of Jerusalem are doing all they can, both in the natural and in the heavenlies, to disrupt this. In other words, behind the scenes, as if a curtain has been pulled back, we are seeing spiritual warfare. We are seeing what Ephesians 6:12 talks about. "*For our struggle is not* against *flesh and blood, but against the rulers, against the powers, against the world forces of this darkness, against the spiritual forces of wickedness in the heavenly places.*"

Imagine principalities, powers, angels, devils, the forces of good, the forces of evil all clashing together in that realm that mercifully, God hides from our view. And so we see that Daniel's prayers cause angels to leave their heaven and come to earth in answer to a man deemed to be "esteemed" by one of those angels. As a result, the enemy's plan fails. So even praying about a promise that God made can be delayed.

Perhaps the most significant thing in these verses is what the angel says to him in verse 12. **As soon as Daniel started praying, his words were heard**. Daniel continues to pray and fast for twenty-one days because there is no answer, no change to the situation. Daniel's prayer has been hijacked, but he doesn't know it! Even so, he remains faithful; he remains in prayer. It didn't take twenty-one days for Daniel's prayers to be heard; it took twenty-one days for his prayers to be answered, because of spiritual warfare!

We've seen Mary and Martha waiting for ten days before they received their answer to prayer; Daniel waiting twenty-one days before his answer came. How about you? Still waiting? How long has it been? Weeks? Months? Years? God's timing in matters of prayer is unknown to us, but we do know the reason for His timing. In John 11:4, Jesus tells us, "*This sickness is not to end in death,* ***but for the glory of God, so that the Son of God may be glorified by it***" (emphasis added).

While we don't know when our prayers will be answered, we can rest assured that God will use our situation to bring glory to Himself. I kind of like that.

What we don't know is how much of a fight the enemy will mount. Mighty but invisible battles are being fought between the powers of light and the powers of darkness all the time. When you kneel to pray, all manner of evil is released to block the outcome of your prayer. Satan's mission is to destroy Christ and His church, by destroying you and me. He's not interested in giving you a flesh wound; he wants to defeat you in areas that will cripple you mentally, physically, and financially. He wants to destroy your worship, your faith, and your support mechanisms. He wants your children and your family in ruins. (Read the book of Job sometime.)

This event in Daniel shows us that when we pray, we engage the angels of heaven. The battle becomes theirs. We're not equipped to enter those frays; we *are* equipped for prayer and holiness—two of Satan's greatest enemies!

Perhaps, if in your dismay at the evil mounted up against you, this wonderful story of hope in 2 Kings 6:14–17 will give you some peace. The king of Aram (a region in central Syria, which includes the current day city of Aleppo, stretching from the mountains of Lebanon eastward past the Euphrates River) was at war with Israel and planning to mount an attack when he learned that Elisha knew every word he spoke, every plan he made; or as the Bible says, "He knows the very words that are spoken in your bedroom". So this king decides to put the invasion of Israel on hold and instead go after Elisha who is in the city of Dothan to kill him.

We can pick up the story in verse 14:

> *He sent horses and chariots and a great army there, and they came by night and surrounded the city. Now when the attendant of the man of God (Elisha) had risen early and gone out, behold, an army with horses and chariots was circling the city. And his servant said to him, "Alas, my master! What shall we do?" So he answered, "**Do not fear, for those who are with us are more than those who are with them.**" Then Elisha prayed and said, "O Lord, I pray, open his eyes that he may see." And the Lord opened the servant's eyes and he saw; and behold, the mountain was full of horses and chariots of fire all around Elisha.* (2 Kings 6:14–17; emphasis mine)

Please go back and read Psalm 91:11.

We need to be aware that all Christians are in a battle and all Christians have an enemy that hates them, and it's so important that our spiritual eyes be opened. "*The thief,*" Jesus said, "*comes only to steal, kill and destroy. I came that they may have life and have it abundantly*" (John 10:10).

A Pastor in Trouble

Several years ago, I was leading worship at a church whose pastor was the godliest man I had ever met. I was fortunate to be able to have a weekly Bible study with him and when we sat together in his office, one on one, I couldn't help but notice and feel the overwhelming presence of God in the room (See Foreword).

One Sunday, as my wife and I listened to him deliver the sermon, he paused as if grasping for the right words or phrase to use. I knew immediately he was struggling—physically, I presumed—and went directly into prayer for him. As I was praying, he, still speechless, slowly looked over at me, and I could see the desperation in his eyes. I nodded to him somehow knowing that he was asking, and I was confirming that I was calling on God to deliver him. He recovered and completed the sermon, but the interlude of his silence was frightening. Later after the service, he told me that Satan had completely attacked him and his mind went blank, and all he could do was look at me knowing that I would be praying for him. He mentioned that Satan attacked him every Sunday morning before the church service.

When he told me that I really lost it. I could feel every instinct of protection rising up within me. "Satan is not going to have my pastor," I told him. "This is going to stop right now."

You know, when you see someone you love and respect being hurt, it's normal to jump in, to go to their defense. I ended up putting my whole being between him and Satan. I began praying for him. There was an intensity to my prayer life. I prayed insistently, then incessantly, and always stubbornly for my pastor's deliverance from these attacks of evil. Several years later, when I asked him to proofread this manuscript, he told me that God had revealed to him that there was fear in every cell of his body because of severe beatings as a young boy from his stepdad. He told me that Satan had used his childhood to fill him with uncertainty and a lack of confidence. He humbled me by telling me that God had told him that it was my intercession that began the healing. Over time and after much prayer, God did heal him. He was fifty-nine years old at the time. Deliverance took forty-nine years! How long did you say you've been waiting?

Just like Elisha and his servant, we are surrounded by a heavenly host of angels willing to go into battle to protect us. And just like the servant, we need to pray for spiritual enlightenment and wisdom so that our response to danger or bad news isn't like the servant, "*Alas my Lord, what shall I do?*" Let it be more like Elisha's response, "***O Lord, let my eyes be opened so that I will not lack assurance of your presence.***"

In 2 Corinthians 10: 3–4, Paul says, "*For though we walk in the flesh, we do not war according to the flesh, for the weapons of our warfare are not of the flesh, but divinely powerful for the destruction of fortresses.*"

Our battle with unanswered prayer, with a life that seems to be upside down, and a target for the enemy is a battle that requires the weapons mentioned by Paul above. Before I address these weapons, let's look at 1 Peter 5:8. "*Be of sober spirit, be on the alert. Your adversary, the devil, prowls around like a roaring lion, seeking someone to devour.*"

The good news is that Satan comes at you with all kinds of noise (like a roaring lion). He brings chaos, desperation, depression, anger, rebellion, and resignation. That means it's impossible for him to sneak up on a child of God.

As if that's not enough, here's what happened in Job 1: "*Now there was a day when the sons of God came to present themselves before the Lord, and Satan also came among them. The Lord said to Satan, 'From where do you come?' Then Satan answered the Lord and said, 'From roaming about on the earth and walking around on it*" (Job 1:6–7).

There's no doubt that Satan, called the Prince of the Air, can hassle you, but God gives you this incredible release from Satan's grip: "*Submit therefore to God. Resist the devil and* ***he will flee from you***" (James 4:7; emphasis mine).

The weapons mentioned in 2 Corinthians 10:4 are the word of God and prayer. It is impossible for Satan to stay around you when you are praising the name of Jesus, confirming that He is your Lord and Savior. We will look at the beating that Christ heaped on Satan in chapter 9 when we look at Intercessory Prayer.

More Devastation

Obviously, Satan attacks all mankind, but the following stats published by Maranatha Life, Donna, Texas, raised my awareness level to the issues that pastors have. They are faced with more work, more problems, and more stress than any other time in the history of the church, and it is taking a frightening toll on the ministry, shown by the statistics below:

- Fifteen hundred pastors leave the ministry each month due to moral failure, spiritual burnout, or contention in their churches.
- Four thousand new churches begin each year, but over seven thousand churches close.
- Fifty percent of pastors' marriages will end in divorce.
- Eighty percent of pastors and 84 percent of their spouses feel unqualified and discouraged in their role as pastors.
- Fifty percent of pastors are so discouraged that they would leave the ministry if they could but have no other way of making a living.
- Eighty percent of seminary and Bible school graduates who enter the ministry will leave the ministry within the first five years. Ninety percent of pastors said their seminary or Bible school training did only a fair to poor job preparing them for ministry.

- Eighty-five percent of pastors said their greatest problem is they are sick and tired of dealing with problem people, such as disgruntled elders, deacons, worship leaders, worship teams, board members, and associate pastors. Ninety percent said the hardest thing about ministry is dealing with uncooperative people.
- Seventy percent of pastors feel grossly underpaid.
- Ninety percent said the ministry was completely different than what they thought it would be before they entered into training.
- Seventy percent felt God called them to pastoral ministry before their ministry began, but after three years of ministry, only 50 percent still felt called.

Pastors' Wives:

- Eighty percent of pastors' spouses feel their spouse is overworked.
- Eighty percent of pastor' wives feel left out and unappreciated by the church members.
- Eighty percent of pastors' spouses wish their spouse would choose another profession.
- Eighty percent of pastors' wives feel pressured to do things and to be something in the church that they are really not.
- The majority of pastor's wives surveyed said that the most destructive event that has occurred in their marriage and family was the day they entered the ministry.

Pastors' Marriages:

- Seventy percent of pastors constantly fight depression.
- Almost 40 percent polled said they have had an extra-marital affair since beginning their ministry.

Pastors' Children:

- Eighty percent of adult children of pastors surveyed have had to seek professional help for depression.

Pastors' Relationships with the Lord:

- Seventy percent of pastors do not have a close friend, confidant, or mentor.
- Ninety-five percent of pastors do not regularly pray with their spouses.
- Eighty percent of pastors surveyed spend less than fifteen minutes a day in prayer.
- Seventy percent said the only time they spend studying the Word is when they are preparing their sermons.

Satan Wants You to Quit

Back in the nineties, I was leading two Bible studies at the company I worked for. In my Thursday morning study, I had told my classmates that anyone connected to preaching the word of God would be subject to an attack by Satan, because that's the last thing the evil one wants. That Sunday, Mother's Day, I came out of church and was feeling somewhat faint, so instead of going out for lunch to celebrate with my wife and mom, I asked if we could just go home. By two o'clock, the paramedics were rushing me to hospital. I was diagnosed with pancreatitis. My blood pressure was 60/40 and all I remember as I lay in the ER was that my feet were elevated to maintain blood flow to my head.

I was in the hospital for two and a half days. On the day I was released, I went directly to my church and had the pastors pray over me and lay hands on me. At the altar that afternoon, I told Satan that I wasn't quitting—that I would work even harder on my Bible studies. There were eight people in that class: five were Christians. The other three accepted the Lord before the study ended.

So how do we storm the invisible citadels and attack the unseen powers?

Here's what Ephesians 6:13–17 has to say. Paul goes to great lengths to tell us how to dress for the battles against demonic forces.

- Put on the full armor of God
- Gird your loins with truth

- Wear the Breastplate of righteousness
- Having shod your feet with the preparation of the gospel of peace.
- Use the shield of faith
- Put on the helmet of salvation
- Employ the Sword of the spirit. (Read your Bible.)

Okay, Paul, I'm all dressed. I'm ready to fight! My adrenalin is flowing! The armor's in place! Put me in, coach!

And what does Paul say? **Pray!** Look at verse 18: "***With all prayer and petition pray at all times*** *in the Spirit and with this in view, be on the alert with all perseverance and petition for all the saints*" (emphasis added). According to Paul, it's that simple: pray!

An Exorcism

It seemed like I could never have a relaxed, loving relationship with my mom. Even on good days, something would happen to cause unrest. Then she was diagnosed with two brain tumors, and her condition slowly deteriorated to the point where she was unable to write. It was just scribble. One day, during one of my Bible studies at work, I invited my pastor to deliver the study on Romans 8. He asked how my mom was doing and I said, "Well, let's call her and ask her." She really liked our pastor, and I knew this phone call would cheer her up.

When she answered, I was stunned to hear her in so much distress. She was crying and panicked and kept repeating, "I don't know what's happening to me. I don't know what's happening to me."

The pastor and I decided to drive over and see her and when we arrived, we found her in really bad shape. It was impossible to quiet her down and to stop her sobbing. Pastor stood to her right, and I knelt on the carpet at her feet holding her trembling hands in her lap as we prayed peace over her.

She got worse! She was completely out of control. Then the pastor spoke sharply to her, I thought he was scolding her. I heard him say, "*In the name of Jesus Christ!*" She became so still, I thought she had died. I looked up at her face and saw tranquility. Within three or four minutes, she was laughing and walking the pastor around her home, showing him all her pictures on the walls and all the stories that went with them. I hadn't seen her this happy in years.

On the way back to my office, as we were discussing her sudden change, my pastor told me that he had felt the presence of evil in her and had commanded it to leave. He told me, gesturing with his hands, "There was a dark form right there next to her, and it moved from there over to the window, paused and disappeared out the window."

My mom lived nine more months and despite increasing pain from her tumors, never complained and had the sweetest disposition from that moment until her passing. I had witnessed an exorcism. Looking back, I realized that I had been no more than two feet from pure evil. But then I realized that I was even closer to the almighty power of God!

The Christian life is a life of conflict. We are at war. Six times in the "warfare passage" of Ephesians 6:11–12, Paul uses the word *against*—a word referring to hand-to-hand combat emphasizing both the intensity of the battle and the personal nature of the fight. The believer's enemies are the demonic hosts of Satan, always assembled for mortal combat.

Even though this chapter discussed the evil forces that are ready to hijack your life and your prayers, I want to make sure you do understand and concentrate on the passage we read from 2 Kings 6:14–17 and Elisha's statement: "***Do not fear, for those who are with us are more than those who are with them.***" Angels are mentioned 273 times in the Bible: 108 times in the Old Testament and 165 times in the New Testament. Please remember, evil is dispatched through prayer and by reading the word of God—Satan's biggest enemies. But nevertheless, evil and demonic forces can put you and your prayer life into a holding pattern. Be patient, be knowledgeable and be persistent, just like Daniel.

Something to Think About:

Many Christians pray out of a sense of habit or duty and don't really expect any answers, especially when it comes to healing. But think about this: if your prayers stir up the demonic forces of evil in an attempt to cut them off, as we saw in Daniel, then you can take comfort in knowing that if they are a threat to Satan, you can be assured they are important to God.

4

God's Sovereignty, God's Will... So Why Bother?

In the last chapter, we looked at how our prayers release the spirit world to go into battle in the heavenlies. I mentioned that we are so fortunate not to see these battles because they are extremely violent and quite frankly, our minds would be seriously impaired if we were visual participants. We do, however, feel the impact. Depending on how the battle is raging, we see delayed answers to the issues we have prayed for. We have also seen in Daniel why it is important to continue in prayer. This chapter will explore one of the ***good spirits*** that is released when we pray.

There Is Powerful Help for Your Prayer Life

God is worthy of receiving quality time from us. I have trouble giving that to Him at times. If I held a conversation with people similar to the interrupted, disconnected, and disjointed prayers I have with God, they would walk away wondering what on earth I was babbling about.

It's easy to come to God unprepared to pray. There are times when my mind just can't shut off the day's events, and it's hard to get it stopped; I can be praying for one thing and unrelated thoughts pop up at all the wrong times; one prayer will lead to reminders of other issues, and I start thinking (not praying) about those.

The thing we don't realize is that God knows before we pray what we are struggling with. Let's look at scripture.

Look with me at Romans 8:26, "*In the same way the Spirit also helps our weakness; for we do not know how to pray as we should,* ***but the Spirit Himself intercedes for us with groanings too deep for words***" (emphasis added). Here is that good spirit mentioned above—the Holy Spirit. Christ promised He would send a Comforter and a Helper, and one of the things He does extremely well is represent the thoughts and needs of our heart directly to the throne of God.

I want to share a story with you that I used in a deacon meeting several years ago, and I admit that I cannot find the book or the author who first wrote it so that I can give him proper credit. Obviously, I wrote it down and saved it in my Word file but erred in not noting the author at the time. Let me repeat it just as I did back then because I can't capture the essence of this story without just restating it to you. The writer is a pastor attending a Sunday evening meal at his church.

> "So this particular time I was talking with a woman whose son had recently been put in jail. She felt that he had been treated very poorly by the police and that the charges against him were unjust. She was angry with the police and anxious about the upcoming trial where she would testify on her son's behalf. After hearing more about her situation I offered to pray for her and her son, which she welcomed. Not knowing quite what to say, and *not wanting to pray anything too specific, or make any requests that God might not answer*

> *and thus disappoint her and me, I focused on praying for peace for them and that they would be able to accept whatever came about.* This is a wonderful prayer in many circumstances and one I've found helpful for myself many times, and it was what I had to offer in this case."

Let me interject for a minute and meet the expression, "*God's will*," head on. This is so much like I used to be. Perhaps it's where your prayer life is: "*Not knowing quite what to say, and* ***not wanting to pray anything too specific, or make any requests that God might not answer and thus disappoint yourself and others***," etc., etc., Do you know how most of us who pray like this usually end our prayers? We give ourselves an out. Actually, we give God an out. Because we don't know what God's will is for the situation, and we don't want to get too far out on a limb and look bad if what we prayed for doesn't happen, we say, "*If it be your will, Lord.*"

Of course, God's will is *more than likely going to prevail* (I'll explain later in the chapters on intercession), and we should pray constantly that it does prevail because He has told us in Romans 8:28: "*And we know that God causes all things to work together for good to those who love God, to those who are called according to His purpose.*"

But there's another side to "if it be your will, Lord."

- For some, it's just a way of not engaging; of not putting their faith out there to be tested and strengthened. It is the perfect expression to cover up their lack of faith.
- We don't know what God's will for a particular situation is, so in these cases, for me, if I'm praying, I want to pray for the miracle. I want to pray for the biggest and best outcome possible!
- For others, for all of us really, it's the most sincere form of submission to God that we could offer.

When we get to the chapter on intercession, we'll talk more about this, but for now, I just want to encourage you to be fully engaged and committed with your prayer life. Never be afraid of going out on a limb as long as you have a scripture to support what you are saying.

Let me finish this story of the woman and her pastor. Listen to the difference in the woman's prayer:

> "I then asked her if she would like to pray. She knew exactly what she wanted to pray for. *She prayed for justice to be done, for her son's innocence to be validated, for her own words in court to be heard and prevail, and for them to be delivered from this trial.* As soon as she began praying, her words reminded me of the many Psalms that cry out for similar kinds of deliverance. I wasn't sure what my prayer reminded me of."

Romans 8:22–23 sums it up for us, "*For we know that the whole creation groans and suffers the pains of childbirth together until now. And not only this, but also we ourselves, having the first fruits of the Spirit, even* ***we ourselves groan within ourselves*** *waiting eagerly for our adoption as sons, the redemption of our body*" (emphasis added), and as we just read in Romans 8:26, "*But the Spirit Himself intercedes for us with groanings too deep for words.*"

That's what this woman was doing. Perhaps some of you have similarly linked your groans with those of the Holy Spirit. These are the groans that can't be contained because they represent such deep loss or such deep need. Most of us try to move God by bargaining with Him; by choosing our words so carefully that we aren't even sure what we've prayed for. Let me tell you loud and clear, God prefers humility to positioning; honesty to posturing. When you dance around trying to get God to do something for you, He sees right through you. It's better to groan and align with the Holy Spirit than to be coy and use your "works" to bypass the Holy Spirit.

You Won't Be the First in History to Groan

Scripture reveals similar acts of communication through groans between humanity and God's Spirit. Exodus 1 says, "*The Egyptians became ruthless in imposing tasks on the Israelites, and made their lives bitter with hard service in mortar and brick and in every kind of field labor. They were ruthless in all the tasks they imposed on them*" (Exod. 1:12–14). Having no one to defend them, the Israelites do the only thing they feel they have power to do: "God, this isn't good here. We're really oppressed. ***If it be your will, can you get us out of here?***"

No. That didn't happen.

What did happen is revealed in Exodus 2: "*And the sons of Israel sighed because of the bondage and they cried out; and their cry for help because of their bondage rose up to God. So God heard their* ***groaning****, and God remembered His covenant with Abraham, Isaac, and Jacob. God saw the sons of Israel, and God took notice of them*" (Exod. 2:23–25). You know the rest of the Exodus story.

Back to our pastor's story:

> "So I think that part of what caught my attention in the prayer of this woman at Community Meal was that *I sensed that I was in the presence of the cry, in the presence of the groan;* and I wasn't ready for it. I was trying to come up with a way to offer words that *asked for something, but not too much.* Words that gave comfort, but also hope. Words that recognize that God is present with us but doesn't always bring about the results that we would like to see, *so we shouldn't get our hopes up too much.*
>
> And she just let out a groan, pretty much bypassing all my careful calculations as to what made for a good prayer at that moment, and letting whatever words formed in her heart be what she had to offer."

Praying the Groan

There are many ways to pray, but maybe one way that we need to explore more is this kind of prayer, even though it makes us vulnerable. This woman, in her prayer, gave no quarter to "*God's will*". Call it a **prayer of desire, a prayer of longing, a prayer of outrage, or a prayer of mourning**, the initial prayer act that puts our spirits in sync with the Spirit of God happens through "sighs too deep for words," and that's all that needs to happen for prayer to be prayer.

I was in a prayer meeting a few years ago, and we were going through the names and needs from the church prayer list. The name of an individual who was a single amputee came up. Now this person also suffered blood clots in his good leg and the doctors pressed him to amputate it, but he refused adamantly! When one of our deacons and a prominent member of our church addressed this prayer request, he started like this: "*Heavenly Father, we just bring to you 'John Doe'* ***who as you know will never get better...***"

It took every ounce of restraint for me not to leap across the table and give this individual a piece of my mind. (Don't send letters or e-mails, I've already asked for forgiveness.) My point is that this is exactly what the pastor in our story was doing; not asking for anything radical. After all, we don't want any miracles breaking out, do we?

So for me, the question becomes, "*At what point do our prayers intersect with the sovereignty and will of God?*" How do our prayers augment, diminish, or somehow change God's will?

As He Is, So Are We in This World (1 John 4:17)

Do you remember chapter 1 where Adam was created to be God's administrator, God's representative, God's intercession on earth? That means that God wanted to accomplish things on earth through Adam. God listened to Adam, did things for and with Adam. Adam had the ability or the connection to have his wishes intersect with God's will because they were both so similar and close to each other. To use the vernacular, they were "on the same page." Since Adam was representing God, we have to assume that God had an interest in and took notice of Adam's thoughts and ideas. If He didn't, then there was no partnership after all. And there won't be with us either.

Consider this: Adam was completely without sin when he was created (as was Eve). But both of them were allowed to have choices, and both of them chose to disobey God. The sin nature entered mankind. Aha, you say… there goes the intersection of our prayers and God's will. Sin has removed all of that!

Not so fast. When Christ took your sin on the cross; your past sins, your present sins, and your future sins; *you* became *without* sin. The book of Romans 5 says,

> *So then as through one transgression (Adam) there resulted condemnation to all men, even so through one act of righteousness (Christ) there resulted justification of life to all men. For as through the one man's disobedience the many were made sinners, even so through the obedience of the One, the many will be made righteous.* (Rom. 5:18–19)

We are now, through Jesus's finished work on the cross, just as sin-free as was Adam when God created him. We are a *new creation.* We are the righteousness of God! Do we still have the choice to sin? Yes! Are those sins forgiven? Yes! Are they forgotten? Hebrews 8:12 says, "*For I will be merciful to their iniquities, and I will remember their sins no more.*"

This is part of the New Covenant we have with God through His Son, Jesus Christ. We are just as able, allowed, permitted, and expected to petition God with our communications (prayers) as was Adam. Not only can our prayers intersect with God's will, He also expects them to! We are the new Adam. We are God's new managers, representatives, and intercessors for the things that take place on earth. We are His new partners!

Listen, I understand; we have all struggled with having our prayers answered exactly the way we have prayed for. **Jim Cymbala** in his book, *The Life God Blesses*, puts it this way: "*There is an ever-present tension between the greatness of God's promises and the still unchanged situations we face after we pray.*"[6] Why is that? The easy answer is this. The one thing that separates us from God is that He *is* God and we *aren't.* God's timing and planning and bringing things together for His glory trump anything and everything we think, do or hope for. Does that mean we shouldn't ask for things then? Things like wisdom, healing, prosperity, freedom from bondage? Absolutely not!

For me, I believe that everything I pray for is within His will. There's a neat passage in Romans that should settle the "*will*" thing forever in your mind and free you up to pray for anything you like. Romans 8:27 (parentheses are mine), "*And He (God) who searches the hearts (ours) knows what the mind of the Spirit is, because He (the Spirit) intercedes for the saints (us) according to the will of God.*" I hope the parentheses didn't throw you off; but seriously, if you didn't get that verse the first time, you need to read it until you do get it. This verse tells us that those groanings that the Spirit issues that are too deep for words when He intercedes for us (Rom. 8:26) are precisely our prayers reformatted to conform to the will of God. No matter what you pray for—healing from cancer, a better job, your kids to get off drugs, etc.—everything is taken to God by the Holy Spirit in accordance with God's will. You never have to temper your petitions with phrases like "*If it be your will, Lord*" ever again. The Holy Spirit takes care of that for you. You are released from the chains that have held you back. I have an expression by Billy Graham on my website that should put some of this into perspective for you: "***Heaven is full of blessings that have never been prayed for***."

I believe that if I pray in Spirit and Truth (faith and fact) and pray *within God's word*, then I am praying *within God's will.* I believe that if I claim a scripture and use it in my intercessions, God honors that and realizes that this is a scripture that He uttered. For example, if I'm praying for healing, I use the scripture in Jeremiah 32:27, "*Behold I am the Lord, the God of all flesh. Is anything too difficult for Me?*"

It's kind of my little reminder to Him. I also believe that God lets me know when He has released me from praying for a situation. As I mentioned earlier, my prayers will always err on the side of a miracle. As we have seen in the Daniel and Lazarus stories, answers to prayer can take time and can test our resolve. Let's visit James 1: "*Consider it all joy, my brethren, when you encounter various trials, knowing that* ***the testing of your faith produces endurance****. And let endurance have its perfect result, so that you may be perfect and complete, lacking in nothing*" (James 1:2–4; emphasis mine).

When that endurance begins to weaken and you start to doubt that your prayers will be answered as you have requested, James 1:6–7 can strengthen you: "*But he must ask in faith without any doubting, for the one who doubts is like the surf of the sea, driven and tossed by the wind. For that man ought not to expect that he will receive anything from the Lord.*" I don't see any indication here that we are expected to shrink away from our requests because it may not be God's will. In fact, I see just the opposite. God wants us to come to Him in faith; not unlike the way you, as a little boy or girl, would go to your parent or grandparent for things.

Not only does God want us coming to Him in faith, according to the scripture in James, but Christ *chides* us for not asking for more, for not having *enough* faith. Read what Christ says in Matthew 6:30: "*But if God so clothes the grass of the field, which is alive today and tomorrow is thrown into the furnace, will He not much more clothe you?* ***You of little faith!***"

Who among you have ever had to teach your kids to misbehave? Who have ever had to tell their kids to expect or want more birthday presents, more TV time, more hours added to their curfew, more cell phone minutes? These things all come natural to kids. Why? Because they sincerely want more, and they sincerely think that either you will give these things to them, or you will cave in if they persist enough with you. They don't hesitate to ask. Why then when we need healing, a job, or a relationship repaired, why do we shrink back from God because it may not be His will, because He may say no? Our kids ask for outrageous things because they expect us to say yes. Why then do we ask life-changing things of God and expect Him to say no?

I want to look at one more scripture in the book of James but before we do, I just want to mention that the author, James, is the half-brother of Jesus. I have to believe that this guy knows what he is talking about. James is lamenting that we look in all the wrong places, and do all the wrong things, searching for the things we need:

> *You lust and do not have; so you commit murder (most likely means 'hate'). You are envious and cannot obtain; so you fight and quarrel.* ***You do not have because you do not ask****. You ask and do not receive, because you ask with wrong motives, so that you may spend it on your pleasures.* (James 4:2–3; emphasis mine)

Here's a challenge for you if you are *still* hung up on the "*will thing*". If your mind-set is still wondering as you pray if in fact this prayer would be part of God's will. I want you to take some time and read all the Gospels—Matthew, Mark, Luke, and John.

- Write down all of the things Christ did;
- All of the things Christ said,
- All of the things Christ admonished;
- And all of the parables used as a teaching tool.

And when you are finished, try and match up that which Christ has addressed in the gospels to the thing you desperately want or need in your life. I guarantee that you will find it; and when you do, claim that scripture and give it to God every time you pray for this issue. Now you know what Christ will do because He already did it. Now you know Christ's will.

Once you have that list, you will have the "*will of God*", now go ahead in confidence with your prayers!

Arguably, God's greatest desire or *will* is found in the book of Matthew 18:14 where He laments for His creation that "*none should perish*". Are you aware that you would have perished had you not *asked* for salvation? Why are we expected to ask for something that He has already willed, that He desperately wants? In fact, in Christ's teaching of the Lord's Prayer when the disciples asked Him to teach them how to pray, we read in Matthew 6:10, "*Your kingdom come, Your will be done…*" Wait a minute, did I read that right? God has a plan; it's part of His will. Yet we are told to pray that His will would be done? Isn't He planning on doing His will anyway? Just how deep does this partnership with God go if He wants us to pray that *His* will is carried out?

Read on: Proverbs 30:8(c) reads, "*Feed me with the food that is my portion.*" That's similar to "*Give us this day, our daily bread*" (Matt. 6:11). But I don't have to read very much further in Matthew (v. 31–32), which says, "*Do not worry then, saying, 'What will we eat?' or 'What will we drink?' or 'What will we wear for clothing?' For the Gentiles eagerly seek all these things; for your heavenly Father* ***knows that you need all these things.***" Clearly then, we have to ask for things God already knows about, already has a plan for, and already has His will determined. So this should encourage us to ask for anything. If we are to ask for all of these things that we know are God's will, is it such a stretch for us to ask for things when we don't know His will? It seems like God has established a pattern of wanting us to ask.

Somehow, we have to get to a point in our relationship with the Almighty where we come to grips with the fact that even though God could do anything He desires (as in exercising His will), He prefers that His creation share in those decisions and actions. In some mysterious way, coinciding with God's plan for us to participate in this partnership with Him on earth, God's power and blessings and answers to prayer are released when His people get involved. Somehow, even though He plans and wills things to be done, somehow our asking, our participation releases Him to do it. Consider carefully, the following issues:

- God could have solved the whole "sin" thing by not planting the tree of the knowledge of good and evil in the garden of Eden, but He needed man to have boundaries and to recognize that God does have restrictions when He allows free choice.

- God could have given **Abraham and Sarah** a son to fulfill his promise before Abraham got impatient and lay down with Hagar. But He wanted Abraham to persevere and take ownership of God's prophesy and promise to him.
- He could have freed the Israelites from **Egypt**, but He sent **Moses** to do it.
- He could have crushed the idolatrous worship going on in **Nineveh**, but He sent **Jonah** to do it.
- He could have killed **Saul of Tarsus** instead of merely blinding him, but He used Paul to write most of the **New Testament**.
- He could have left you a sinner. But He brought someone or something into your life that changed everything. He heard your cries for salvation and granted them so that you would be part of His Kingdom, reaching out to the lost, bringing others to His redemption.
- He could have sent His angels to free Jesus from the cross, but being a righteous God, He needed to fulfill the law so that you and I could live under grace.

Throughout Scripture, God uses people to get things done, just like we were his partners! Oh, that's right, we've already acknowledged that! And because we ***are*** His partners, working together with Him, side by side, our needs, frailties, and petitions intersect with His will all day long.

The bottom line? Second Chronicles 7:14 tells us that **prayer was always close to God's heart**. "*And My people, who are called by My name humble themselves and pray and seek my face and turn from their wicked ways, then I will hear from heaven, will forgive their sin and will heal their land.*"

That means all the questions and objections surrounding prayer are God's problems. I'm not trying to be cavalier, but the only things I need to know are:

(a) God wants me to pray. Just because I have questions about His ways and His timing doesn't exempt me from being humble and turning to Him in prayer.
(b) God's word gives me examples of being persistent: the neighbor asking his friend for bread in the middle of the night; the woman before the judge. (We will look at these in more detail in later chapters.)
(c) God's word gives me examples of the times His will was changed by petition: David and the angel destroying Jerusalem; Moses on the mountain when God's wrath wanted to wipe out the Israelites. We'll look at these also, a little later in the book.

Even though God has the authority and sovereignty to prevail,

- He doesn't want your prayer life to wither;
- He doesn't want your hope or your spirit quenched.
- And most of all, He doesn't want to lose communication with you.
- **Remember: included in "His Will" is that it's "His Will" that you pray!**

By accepting that God's will is supreme, we are given **complete freedom** to ask anything. Let's review real quick: look again at Romans 8:27: "*And He who searches the hearts knows what the mind of the Spirit is, because He intercedes for the saints according to the will of God.*"

From all this, we learn two things:

1. That fluency in prayer is not essential to praying. The deep, from-the-bottom-of-your-heart groan is filled with meaning, and God understands it, because it matches the passionate hunger of his own Spirit.
2. That we don't ever have to be concerned with tempering our prayers, trying to determine what may or may not be God's will. The Spirit does that for us! We're free to ask **anything** in His name. John 14 is very clear when Christ says, "*Whatever you ask in My name, that will I do, so that*

> *the Father may be glorified in the Son. If you ask Me anything in My name, I will do it*" (John 14:13–14).

For me, if I don't know what the will of God is, I'm going for the gold. I'm asking for the miracle. I'm asking that God receive the utmost glory by doing something phenomenal. I'm going to pray for restoration, for healing, for whatever the issue demands; until I do know what His will is. I want my faith stretched and tested; because that's the only way it can grow. **I'll be persistent, God can deal with the "will" thing**.

Something to Chew On:

Mankind was never created to die. Think about all of the things you have created - gardens, paintings, music, a toy box for your son, even your children; did you create any of these things expecting them to die or to fall into a state of disrepair? Of course not! Why then, would your heavenly Father not want prosperity, wellness, freedom from anxiety, etc., for you? If you believe that, what's stopping you from asking for it when seasons of trouble come upon you?

5

Build It (Your Prayer Life) and He Will Bless It

Chapter 4 looked at the Sovereignty of God, His will, and the relationship between that and prayer. It's important that you understand, in the final analysis, **God's will is absolute**. Important because you won't respect a God whose decisions are neither black nor white, but grey; important because we need to have an authority figure in our lives whose moral compass, whose plumb line is constant in all circumstances; and important because a God who will be turned and twisted about by emotions will never give us the steady footing we need to conquer life's battles. But don't ever forget about, or give up on God's grace and God's mercy.

A navigator on a sailing vessel in the North Atlantic observed an interesting phenomenon. The prevailing winds at sea level were very definitely from the west at about eighteen knots. But icebergs scattered all about the vessel were drifting in a southwesterly direction! The captain concluded and verified with his navigation charts, that the seven-eighths of the icebergs' mass being under water were all influenced by ocean currents that were flowing in a direction contrary to, and more powerful than, the surface winds. God's will is like this kind of current. Often, we can be influenced to act and seek a direction that is governed by popular opinion or peer pressure, or our own selfish desires (surface winds), when all along, if we are rooted in God's word (deeper currents), we will make wiser decisions; wiser prayer requests, and proceed in a different direction. This story reminds me of a Scripture we have already looked at, but worth repeating: "*But he must ask in faith without any doubting, for the one who doubts is like the surf of the sea, driven and tossed by the wind*" (James 1:6).

In the last chapter, I challenged you to search for God's will by reviewing the four gospels and taking note of the things that Christ addressed during His ministry. Remember also that His ministry was short—just over three years—so Christ had neither the time nor the interest in being superfluous. You will find Christ addressing the following:

- reconciliation (relational issues you may be having)
- adultery (lusts and temptations)
- marriage and divorce
- truthfulness (perjury: yes is yes, and no is no)
- loving your neighbors and your enemies
- tithing
- prayer
- fasting
- finances
- anxiety and worry
- judging others
- and, of course, healing!

So if you are praying parallel to Christ's desires, I guarantee that you will find something in Scripture that He has supported or dismissed and this is the scripture you can claim in your prayers.

If He's going to bless our prayer life, what does God expect of us?

Let's look at what God expects of us because of who we are in Christ. If you agree with me that we are a new creation in Him, then perhaps you will agree that there needs to be some changes made to the old "us". Second Corinthians 3:18 says this: "*But we all, with unveiled face, **beholding as in a mirror the glory of the Lord**, are being **transformed** into the **same** image from glory to glory, just as from the Lord, the Spirit*" (emphasis added).

As we move along this path of becoming more Christlike, we begin to enter into the Holiness of God. This happens when we nourish the Holy Spirit which dwells within us. First John 2 shows us how we receive and accept that transformation:

> *But you have an anointing from the Holy One, and you all know... as for you, the anointing which you received from Him abides in you, and you have no need for anyone to teach you; but as His anointing teaches you about all things, and is true and is not a lie, and just as it taught you, you abide in Him.* (1 John 2:20, 27)

Just to be clear where this Holy Spirit, this Teacher comes from I want to quote one more Scripture, Christ speaking: "*But the Helper, the Holy Spirit, **whom the Father will send in My name**, He will teach you all things, and bring to your remembrance all that I said to you*" (John 14:26; emphasis mine).

Christians then are on this path of becoming more Christlike, more holy, more Spirit-filled, and more knowledgeable and aware through the teaching of the Holy Spirit. Since we are becoming more like Christ, we should know what standard God set for Him when He entered into His ministry. The very first words we read from Christ appear in Matthew 3:15. In a barren wasteland along the western shores of the Dead Sea, John the Baptist was baptizing many from Jerusalem, Judea and the district around the Jordan River. As Christ approached, to be baptized, John tried to prevent Him saying that *he* needed to be immersed by Christ. Here's what our Lord said,

"Permit it at this time; for in this way it is fitting for us to fulfill all righteousness."

Let's walk this back so that we can get a full understanding of what's happening here and a full understanding of where we are heading as we become more like Him. First of all, why would Christ need to be baptized? Part of the act of being baptized involved repentance. What could Christ possibly have to repent? Absolutely nothing! But there's more to this than nothing; Jewish customs (as given by God), Jewish Laws (also given by God), and the fact that Jesus was born as a man—just like you and I, all need to be addressed.

Christ was circumcised at birth and observed all the other Jewish customs as well as the ordinances of the Law of Moses, not with a view to his own justification, but to fulfill the mission committed to him by the Lord, and God of all things.

Consider this: the God of all creation has come to earth. In every corner of the universe, there is not one thing left to be created; it's all been done. There is not one thing for Christ to acquire; He has everything. His mission is to live every second of His earthly life in moral excellence, waiting on God His Father, so that all who observe Him will have a perfect example to follow. Anything other than excellence would cause people to stumble, to go astray, and to question God's own righteousness. Christ recognizes that nearly all of humanity will walk through this life seeking an earthly reward for their lifestyle. Yet His life, fulfilling all righteousness, will have no ulterior motives for gain other than attracting mankind to try to live in a similar fashion.

The eighteenth chapter of Ezekiel addresses the idea that a father's sins are not judged against the son. Instead, **individual accountability** is stressed. Ezekiel 18:19 says, "*When the son has practiced justice and righteousness and has observed all My statutes and done them, he shall surely live;*" **18:21** goes on, "*But if the wicked man turns from all his sins which he has committed and observes all My statutes and practices justice and righteousness, he shall surely live; he shall not die.*" While these Scriptures apply more to us than to Christ, as we turn from our sinful ways, we have to see the parallels in Christ's life; this is His purpose; not to confess sin, because He was sinless; but in acting as a man, to practice justice, practice and reflect righteousness and, most importantly, for our salvation, to fulfill the law.

Hebrew 4:14 reveals Christ's ultimate status of priesthood, conferred by God: "*Therefore, since we have a great high priest who has passed through the heavens, Jesus the Son of God, let us hold fast our confession.*" In order to become this high priest, the Mosaic laws and precepts must be fulfilled. The Jewish high priests were accepted into office through washing and anointing; and so must be the case for Christ, for He is to become the High Priest of the House of God. Therefore, circumcised at birth, He now must be baptized, washed, and blessed by the Holy Spirit. In fulfilling these things, He was now ready, as High Priest to proceed with His mission—to be the sacrificial lamb; to take on the sins of the world. Christ will walk in full righteousness, fully recognized as a High Priest, to set an example for mankind, and to reclaim man from the abyss that Adam set in motion.

This is what God expected from His Son. As we live in Him and Him in us, the expectations for ourselves should aspire to the same level. And so while Christ fulfilled the law; we can fulfill His grace. The people He mingled with couldn't fulfill the law, and neither can we. But we can live a righteous life under grace because that's how God sees us, through His Son.

Back to our question: What does God expect of us?

Let's look at 2 Chronicles 7:

> *If I shut up the heavens so that there is no rain, or if I command the locust to devour the land, or if I send pestilence among* ***My people****, and My people who are called by* ***My name humble*** *themselves and* ***pray*** *and* ***seek My face*** *and* ***turn from their wicked ways****, then I will hear from heaven, will forgive their sin and will heal their land.* (2 Chron. 7:13–14; emphasis mine)

In today's vernacular, verse 13 *could* read like this: "If your world falls apart: you lose your job, lose your home, your relationships tank, you become stricken by illness or disease or you succumb to an addiction", then God says in verse 14, "Here's what I want you to do…" Let's examine this verse by asking, **what are the five things** God asks of us in order to please Him?

(A) **My people**, called by **My name**.

Don't take this too lightly. According to God, Jews are the Chosen People (Isa. 45:4 and Isa. 65:9) because they were chosen to make the idea of **one God known to the world**. It certainly was not because the Israelites were a mighty nation. In fact, Deuteronomy 7:7 states, "*It is not because you are numerous that God chose you, indeed you are the smallest of people.*" Though a nation with a massive standing army may have been the more logical choice to **spread the word of God**, the success of such a mighty people would have been attributed to ***their*** strength, not the power of God.

Just like the Jews, we Christians are now responsible to spread the "Good News". We are the disciples now. We are the new twelve. If Our Lord, in only three and a half years, could trust His entire plan to be set forth by only twelve devotees, one would think He can rely on the 2.2 billion worldwide, who claim to be Christians. That's one third of the world's population! We should be making a bigger dent, don't you think?

Just like the Jews, we are not the largest religious force; and just like the Jews, it's not about our strength but about our love by which the Gospel is spread.

Remember Adam's role—to be His representative, His shadow, His illusion; to carry the weight and authority of His glory. There used to be a bumper sticker: "If you were on trial for being a Christian; would there be enough evidence to convict you?" That's something to think about! Image is everything!

Many years ago, when I was working in a plastics plant in Canada, our sales and marketing people had finally, after several years, persuaded Coca-Cola in Atlanta to give us a trial order of our Styrofoam cups with Coke's logo on it. It seemed almost impossible to please them. The color wasn't just right; the logo was too low on the cup; then it was too high. It seemed like we would never get their approval. One day, one of their representatives came to our plant just outside of Toronto to inspect our process. In a meeting in the marketing office, he saw some hand-drawn mock-ups our people had been using to position the blanket that transferred the color to the cup. They were even colored with red pencil but in fact were a really bad representation of Coke's actual logo. The visitor from Coke ordered us to shred every single drawing and diagram in the entire plant. Apparently, there was a law at the time that any logo that was misrepresented by a drawing could be used by a competitor to break the trademark the logo carried. In other words, if it wasn't the exact "trademarked" logo, it could be taken into court as proof that even the company did not respect its own trademark; and the actual logo could become public domain. It was all about "image" with Coke, and it's even more so with God. "**My People**", "**My Name**", **means everything to God**.

Your prayer life has to acknowledge who you are in God. Imagine a meeting in a lawyer's office to read the last will and testament of a very wealthy individual. Suddenly, someone bursts into the room and says, "I'm his long-lost brother! I deserve to share in the proceeds of the will!" Well, obviously, the man would have to prove his identity to even be considered as an heir.

We are also heirs, but we don't have to prove our identity. Once we have accepted Christ as our Savior, God, unlike the attorneys, is very much aware of our identity. Then *when we come* to Him in prayer to petition His Grace or Mercy or Blessing, *knowing who we are* **(His people)** *in God* gives us the boldness to lay our petitions at His feet.

"*Therefore let us draw near with confidence to the throne of Grace, so that we may receive mercy and find grace to help in time of need*" (Heb. 4:16).

A prayer life built on the confidence of knowing who we are in God and knowing that the throne of God has been opened to us—a sanctuary—will lead us to His Mercy and Grace in our times of need.

(B) **Humility**. "*And My people who are called by My name **humble** themselves.*"

"*Pride goes before destruction, and a haughty spirit before stumbling*" (Prov. 16:18). God is well aware that everything we have and everything we are came from Him. For man to boast in himself is to relegate God's Majesty and His gifts below man's accomplishments.

> *And all of you, clothe yourselves with **humility** toward one another, for God is opposed to the proud, but gives grace to the **humble**. Therefore **humble** yourselves under the mighty hand of God, that He may exalt you at the proper time, casting all your anxiety on Him because He cares for you.* (1 Pet. 5:5–7; emphasis mine)

> *Do nothing from selfishness or empty conceit, but with **humility** of mind, regard one another as more important than yourselves.* (Phil. 2:3; emphasis mine)

Listen to the words of Jesus: "*Whoever exalts himself shall be humbled; and whoever humbles himself shall be exalted*" (Matt. 23:12).

Humility mirrors the condition of your heart. Look at the expressive words from Psalm 51:17: "*The sacrifices of God are a broken spirit; a broken and a contrite heart, O God, You will not despise.*"

In order for God to accept our humility and pardon us by His boundless mercy, He requires that we are truly contrite. There are lasting issues when we deal with guilt, regret, and remorse. You can have regrets and remorse in your life, which lead to an acknowledgement of guilt; but if the guilt remains, then your confession is baseless. The world pounces on this guilt and brings a bondage, a kind of death that you can't shed; but if your repentance leaves you free from regret, then you gain a freedom, a salvation from that act. Psalm 51:17 says that such contrition, such repentance, such brokenness is pleasing to God because of its sincerity and because it releases His people into freedom.

(C) **Devotion**. "*And* ***pray*** *and* ***seek My face***."

"*I love those who love Me; and those who diligently seek Me will find Me*" (Prov. 8:17).

"*Seek the Lord while He may be found; Call upon Him while He is near*" (Isa. 55:6). The three Wise Men sought God and traveled a great distance to worship Him. Wise men today still seek God.

Whenever the clutter of our lives begins to interfere with putting God and His kingdom first, we begin to show our true, previously hidden earthly priorities. What is the first thing on your mind when you wake up in the morning? How about the second thing? Third? As I write this, Alabama is ranked number 1 in the AP college football polls. Previously unranked University of Arizona is now twenty-fourth following a victory over number 18 Oklahoma State. "Wow!" I'm thinking, UofA is the twenty-fourth best team in the country! Well, guess what? The number of things you think about when you wake up ***before*** you think of God is where He is ranked in the standings of your life. At some point, at some "ranking" level, say fourth or fifth, "*devotion*" to God loses its meaning, doesn't it?

Exodus 20 reveals God's heart regarding devotion. "*I am the Lord your God, who brought you out of the land of Egypt, out of the house of slavery. You shall have no other gods before Me*" (Exod. 20:2–3). Leaping to the New Testament continues God's instruction without missing a beat. In Matthew 6, Jesus says, "*No one can serve two masters; for either he will hate the one and love the other, or he will be devoted to one and despise the other. You cannot serve God and wealth*" (Matt. 6:24).

Yeah, but wait a minute, Pastor. I need to provide for my family; I have obligations at work; my bosses have expectations of me. I work hard to provide the level of income that gives us our standard of living; some of those activities come with concerns and anxieties, even worry; and then there are the family issues; time with the kids, my parents, my wife, her parents. It just never lets up, so why shouldn't I strive for wealth so I can provide?

Those are all valid claims my friends, and God Bless you for wanting to make that difference in the life of your family. But take a minute and read Matthew 6:25–34. Jesus knows your schedule better than you do. Verse 33 is especially relevant for you: "*But seek first His kingdom and His righteousness, and all these things will be added to you.*"

Devotion is all about attitude. And this attitude, this point of view, is a reflection of our heart, a reflection of all that we have taken in over time. Devotion! Put God first as often as you can and watch Him make your paths straight.

(D) **Repentance**. "*And* ***turn from their wicked ways****.*"

When God became humanity through His son Jesus Christ, all sinners who desired forgiveness and repented, were sanctified just for the asking. God can't stand sin and views us through the cleansing that Christ provides. Once we have repented, God is ready to do business with us. Jesus addresses this issue often:

> *The time is fulfilled, and the kingdom of God is at hand; repent and believe in the gospel.* (Mark 1:15)

> *I tell you that in the same way, there will be more joy in heaven over one sinner who repents than over ninety nine righteous persons who need no repentance.* (Luke 15:7)

> *Thus it is written, that the Christ would suffer and rise again from the dead the third day, and that repentance for forgiveness of sins would be proclaimed in His name to all the nations, beginning from Jerusalem.* (Luke 24:46–47)

Paul speaks to us in 2 Peter 3:9, "*The Lord is not slow about His promise, as some count slowness, but is patient toward you, not wishing for any to perish but for all to come to repentance.*"

And finally,

> *"Therefore I will judge you, O house of Israel, each according to his conduct," declares the Lord God,*

> *"Repent and turn away from all your transgressions, so that iniquity may not become a stumbling block to you. Cast away from you all your transgressions which you have committed and make yourselves a new heart and a new spirit! For why will you die, O house of Israel?"* (Ezek. 18:30–31)

As we go through the day to day routines of our lives, we may build little kingdoms in our jobs and in our relationships to the point where they account for disproportionate amounts of our dedication, devotion, and time. These are called idols. In any event, we all "*sin and fall short of the glory of God.*" In addition as we sin, we may gossip, form judgments; we might even call someone a name here and there. How often have we yearned or coveted or become jealous over something or someone? We bend the truth; sometimes we just flat out lie. What about embracing "eye candy"? And possibly worse—how we justify it!

These are not sins requiring us to be "**born again**", again. That's not possible. But we can repent. Margaret Thatcher, prime minister of Britain said, "Sometimes you have to win your battles more than once." Frequently we have to repent many times to break old habits.

Here's an Old Testament view of how God tried to warn the Israelites regarding sin:

> *If you obey the Lord your God to keep His commandments and His statutes which are written in this book of the law, if you turn to the Lord your God with all your heart and soul. For this commandment which I command you today is not too difficult for you, nor is it out of reach. It is not in heaven, that you should say, "Who will go up to heaven for us to get it for us and make us hear it, that we may observe it?" Nor is it beyond the sea, that you should say, "Who will cross the sea for us to get it for us and make us hear it, that we may observe it?"* ***But the word is very near you, in your mouth and***

> ***in your heart, that you may observe it. See, I have set before you today life and prosperity, and death and adversity****. In that I command you today to love the Lord your God, to walk in His ways and to keep His commandments and His statutes and His judgments, that you may live and multiply, and that the Lord your God may bless you in the land where you are entering to possess it. But if your heart turns away and you will not obey, but are drawn away and worship other gods and serve them, I declare to you today that you shall surely perish. You shall not prolong your days in the land where you are crossing the Jordan to enter and possess it. I call heaven and earth to witness against you today, that I have set before you life and death, the blessing and the curse.* ***So choose life in order that you may live,*** *you and your descendants.* (Deut. 30:10–19; emphasis mine)

Each of us in our own way are either in some kind of bondage or some kind of exile. And God is saying, "I don't want you living there, missing out on the good things, the blessings; repent and seek life." Is it possible to build a better prayer life without repentance, without actually asking God to forgive our sins? Perhaps this true, short story will put it into perspective.

In 1999, weighing 277 pounds, I suffered a heart attack. I didn't particularly like the doctor who was assigned to me in the hospital, so about a month later, I requested a change and the very first meeting with my new cardiologist went something like this. Doctor (in an excited or animated manner): "*You're one hundred pounds overweight!*" Me (genuinely trying to sound serious): "*Do you recommend the carbohydrate diet or the Atkins' diet?*" Doctor (still animated): "*Listen! If it tastes good, spit it out!*" That answer cracks me up every time I repeat the story. However, even though I have lost about fifty pounds, I'm nervous about every visit to the point where I take my phone off my belt, remove my shoes, wallet, keys, small change, etc. I shed as much weight as possible before I step on the scale outside of his office.

So what's my point in relation to building a better prayer life and confessing sin? Under grace, God has forgiven every sin you ever committed, every sin you are currently committing; and every sin you ever *will* commit. But when you shed your sin before going before God (think weight, before getting on the scale), you *know* you've done everything you could to present the very best of you. You feel better about *you!*

Christians should always remember that Christ has died for *all* our sins, even those we haven't committed yet; but repentance brings a freshening for us. Mankind has a problem with guilt. We struggle to shed it, to wash it away even though God tells us in Hebrews 8:12, "*For I will be merciful to their iniquities, and I will remember their sins no more.*" So when we sin, it's always a good thing for us just to say, "You know what, Lord, I messed up; I'm sorry."

(E) **Prayer**. "*Humble themselves and **pray**.*"

There's a parable in Matthew whereby Christ, looking for nourishment, approaches a fig tree. Normally, both leaves and fruit appear simultaneously in the seasonal cycle of these trees; and although Christ finds leaves, He does not find fruit. He proceeds to wither the tree. The meaning is a message to Israel, a nation that has always been unfruitful despite having every opportunity, every advantage to show the impact of God's long-standing love for her.

Just like Israel, we have all the tools, all the knowledge, all the opportunities and advantages to make a difference. Externally, we appear to be strong Christians (our leaves are in full bloom), but we aren't bearing fruit because we doubt the power of prayer.

Listen to what Christ says following this incident with the fig tree: "*Truly I say to you, if you have faith and do not doubt, you will not only do what was done to the fig tree, but even if you say to this mountain, 'Be taken up and cast into the sea,' it will happen. And all things you ask in prayer, believing, you will receive*" (Matt. 21:21–22).

How many times have you prayed diligently with all of your heart and soul, even groaning like the spirit in Romans, only to have nothing, absolutely nothing happen? Many times, your situation or the one you are praying for, gets worse. And we wonder, "Where are you, Lord?" But God knows our tendency to give up during these periods of quiet. Watch Isaiah 49:14, "*But Zion said, 'The Lord has forsaken me, and the Lord has forgotten me.*"

And God, who is always grieved when His people fail to trust Him, responds immediately (v. 15–16): "*Can a woman forget her nursing child and have no compassion on the son of her womb? Even these may forget but I will not forget you.* ***Behold I have inscribed you on the palms of My hands;*** *your walls are continually before Me.*"

There's no doubt that all of Christianity, all believers, all of us have had certain times or seasons in our lives when:

- We simply didn't know how to pray,
- Or whether to pray at all.
- We have an experience where there are no words right there to express what is going on.
- Situations arise where it is unclear what one is supposed to desire or ask of God.
- There is an extended period of time when the energy for the effort to even try to pray just isn't present.
- Many reading this book may, at some point in their lives have even given up on their prayer life.

After allowing the agony that Christ suffered on the cross, will God now abandon us? Will the nearness of His son at His right hand in heaven, still bearing the scars in His hands, allow God to turn away from our cries?

These are the times, when the waiting, the silence becomes unbearable and these are the times when Satan lays powerful temptations on us. These are the times when our resolve abandons us; yet if we prevail, these are the times when God blesses our faithfulness and blesses our life.

Jesus prepared us for this: "***According to your faith will it be done to you***" (Matt. 9:29). "*Wait on the Lord; be of good courage, and He shall strengthen your heart; wait, I say on the Lord!*" (Ps. 27:14).

George Muller lived in Britain in the 1800s and wanted to show people God's goodness and willingness to answer prayer. He decided to build orphanages to house and feed homeless children. But to show God's blessings, he chose to build these homes without asking anyone but God for assistance. During that time he built The Orphanage campus at Ashley Down, where it is reported that he cared for and educated over 18,000 children. He educated over a hundred thousand more in other schools at the Orphanage's expense and distributed hundreds of thousands of Bibles and countless tracts in addition to supporting hundreds of missionaries. He never ever asked for one penny from anyone. His children never missed a meal, and he never had a debt.

"I live in the spirit of prayer," he said. "I pray as I walk, when I lie down, and when I rise. And the answers are always coming. Tens of thousands of times have my prayers been answered. When once I am persuaded that a thing is right, I go on praying for it. The great point is never to give up till the answer comes. **The great fault of the children of God is, they do not continue in prayer; they do not persevere. If they desire anything for God's glory, they should pray until they get it.**

When it comes to God's timetable, let's not get impatient. Let's stay persistent in prayer. And let's keep looking and expecting an answer, no matter how God chooses to get the job done.

God has a specific time in mind when His promise will be fulfilled. God knows exactly the time and place that "help" will do the most good. God's answer can be "yes" but "*not yet.*"

It is in these times of "not yet" where faith meets promise. God has lots of history on His side of keeping promises, but oftentimes, our faith is inversely proportional to the wait time. Our biggest obstacle when we pray is to ***wait in faith*** until the day of God's favor and salvation. Throughout history man has been searching:

- for new frontiers,
- cures for disease,
- life in outer space,
- knowledge,
- inner peace and

- the real reason for our existence.

Second Chronicles 16:9 reveals another massive search that is timeless and unending: "*For the eyes of the Lord move to and fro throughout the earth that He may strongly support those whose heart is completely His.*" Man sees your personality; God sees your character (Luke 16:15).

God will bless your prayer life if you **build it with humility**, **seek His face through devotion**, **turn your life around through repentance**, and **wait for His day of favor and salvation with patience**.

6

What Matters Most, Your Faith or Your Circumstances?

Does God care more about your faith than your circumstances? God never seems to react the way we want Him to. "*'For My thoughts are not your thoughts, neither are your ways My ways,' declares the Lord*" (Isa. 55:8). His dealings with man sometimes really puzzle us. Has mankind changed since Adam and Eve? I believe we have. Think about the following—how it pertains to your life and what changes you can make.

In the garden, in peace and tranquility, God freely mingled (spiritually) with Adam and Eve, talking to them and teaching them, displaying on a daily basis His omnipotence. Life was pretty uncomplicated; sin was unknown, and there were no in-laws or grandparents. For a time, there weren't even any children. No bosses, no traffic jams, no bills, and not even any Starbucks. God had Adam and Eve's full attention, and vice versa!

Today, in many instances, **God allows storms**—anything but peace and tranquility—to get our attention. You may have purchased this book because there are storms in your life. For the most part, our "*busyness*" as we go through our daily routines sets God on a back burner until we face a situation that we can't control. At this point, our "circumstance" is at a higher level of prominence in our life than our faith has been. Now we turn in earnest to God, to prayer, and to prayer chains. Is it possible that God allowed this "circumstance" to develop to bring us to a greater level of communication, to a deeper relationship with Him?

Can we make an overriding statement that those who expect to grow in their faith should expect storms and difficulties? Is that God's plan? Certainly, faith won't be stretched and tested in periods or seasons of calm. Someone once said, "*No one can climb a smooth mountain.*" But that's a huge stretch to make God the culprit, don't you think? In Matthew 11:30, Christ said, "***My yoke is easy and My burden is light.***" Doesn't sound like a lot of storms there!

Let's look at John 16:33. "***These things I have spoken to you, so that in Me you may have peace. In the world you have tribulation, but take courage; I have overcome the world.***"

So we were born to live in a garden, but our lives resemble living on a freeway at rush hour! Jesus invites us to find His peace so that our lives can return to that "*garden peace*" and "*garden tranquility*" that existed between Adam, Eve, and God. Jesus is saying that our relationship with Him will allow us to get above the worldly storms and tribulations because He did. If you agree with this, then why aren't we at peace? Why is there turmoil in our lives? Why do we spend so much time at the "end of our rope" or with "our nerves on the edge"?

We all have circumstances in our lives. The question is what do we do with them?

From John 16:33 above, "***In Me you may have peace.***" Everyone I've taught this lesson to, and I would guess all of you reading this for the first time, have experienced just how much faith it takes to find peace (or not) in the midst of tribulation.

A former pastor of ours said, "I'd rather be in the boat, in the storm with Jesus, than temporarily safe on shore without Him." This man had found peace. What do we do with *our* circumstances?

- First, we identify which area of our faith needs to be employed. If our circumstance is a health issue, we pull out the "Great Physician" sector. If it's financial, I think we use the prayer of Jabez or the "Great Provider" one; and if it's relational, we assure ourselves that family, friends, and fellowship were all God's idea.
- Then we tell Him in great detail what our concerns and tribulations are as we give them to Him.
- Then within five to ten minutes we take them back from Him and start worrying again.
- Then we wonder, "God, where is the peace you promised?"

Does all of this sound familiar? Are you in a tug of war between your spiritual side and your worldly side for control over which part of you actually has control?

Look with me at Matthew 14. The disciples have departed by boat and have encountered a raging storm threatening to capsize them. They see Christ walking toward them on the water and cry out in fear. Christ tells them:

> ***Take courage, it is I; do not be afraid****. Peter said to Him, "Lord, if it is You, command me to come to You on the water." And He said,* ***"Come!"*** *And Peter got out of the boat, and walked on the water and came toward Jesus. But seeing the wind, he became frightened, and beginning to sink, he cried out, "Lord, save me!" Immediately Jesus stretched out His hand and took hold of him, and said to him, "****You of little faith, why did you doubt?****"* (Matt. 14:27–31; emphasis mine)

When Peter asks Christ to command him to come to Him on the water in verse 28, he does what most of us do during trials and difficulties; we exhibit the weakness of our faith by asking for signs and miracles, as if we don't have enough examples of His omnipotence already.

Peter allowed his circumstances to defeat his faith. When Christ said, "Come!" in verse 29, He was looking at Peter's faith. When Peter stepped out of the boat, he was looking at Christ's grace. Peter gave his circumstances, his fear, and the rolling, violent waves to Christ; and in return, he found peace. That's what He was saying in our previous passage—John 16, by your faith, you will find peace in Me. Peter found that peace—for a few steps—until **he let his circumstances overcome his faith**, and he took them back, just like we do!

When we kneel to pray, God looks first at our heart, then our faith, and then He listens to our prayer. Communicating with God requires a relationship with Him. Second Chronicles 16:9(a), "*For the eyes of the Lord move to and fro throughout the earth that He may strongly support those whose heart is completely His.*" And also 1 Samuel 16:7(b), "*For God sees not as man sees, for man looks at the outward appearance, but the Lord looks at the heart.*"

Let's unpack this a little more. Here's our core statement:

We all have circumstances in our lives. The question is what do we do with them?

First, we put our faith to work.

The first thing we need as we bring our issues to God is **faith**. That's ***our*** will; to have enough faith to believe that our prayers will be answered, that our circumstances will get an audience with God, and that we will find peace.

When we engage our faith, we should have the mind-set that "*this may take a while*". Not because God wants to test you, rather because there are other issues that need to be brought into focus (as we've seen in Daniel and with Jesus and Lazarus), so that God can have the greatest impact and bring Himself the most glory. We should also have the mind-set of "*I can't wait to see how God takes care of this.*" We should be willing to employ perseverance. If answers come sooner than later—great! But perseverance involves praying while waiting.

Unfortunately, we've grown away from the concept of patience. Consider just for a moment the great mariners from Europe; the Magellans, Drakes, Vespuccis, the Captain Cooks, and Christopher Columbuses. And what about Marco Polo? He hasn't always been a swimming pool game. Fast forward from them to the Lewises and Clarks, Daniel Boones, the John Wesley Powells. Imagine waving good-bye to these loved ones as they set off on their adventures. It would take years before any word was received back home about their progress, their safety. But that lifestyle is behind us! We want instant answers now:

- There are just way too many things offered to us in life that hanging around over one thing seems meaningless.
- Does that mean we have become overachievers and multitaskers?
- Have we become a society that simply scratches the surface, attaining no depth before moving on?
- Is shallowness the end result of our "fast-food" lifestyle?

Speaking of lifestyles, just look at our lives: we cook faster, travel faster, produce things faster, spend our resources faster, and we let these routines invade our prayer lives and we expect God to "keep up".

We're into microwaving, God is into marinating.

Our prayer lives may be like the **African Cheetah** who has to run down his prey to eat. He certainly has the tools because he can reach speeds of seventy miles per hour. But there's a problem. The cheetah's heart in undersized for his body, and he tires quickly. So if he doesn't catch his supper early, he has to give up the chase.[7] We're somewhat the same way.

- We get the prayer request,
- Race to the rescue with a wonderful prayer,

- But because we don't have the heart to persevere, we quit—way too early!
- And we too, just like the cheetah, go away hungry and disillusioned.

There's little doubt that persevering and patience require faith. We believe, but sometimes we weaken and give up our fight.

On the night that Judas betrayed Our Lord in the garden, an interesting series of events took place. They are recorded in Matthew 26:

> *Then Jesus came with them to a place called Gethsemane, and said to His disciples, "**Sit here while I go over there and pray**." And He took with Him Peter and the two sons of Zebedee, and began to be grieved and distressed. Then He said to them, "**My soul is deeply grieved, to the point of death; remain here and keep watch with Me**." And He went a little beyond them, and fell on His face and prayed, saying, "**My Father, if it is possible, let this cup pass from Me; yet not as I will, but as You will**." And He came to the disciples and found them sleeping, and said to Peter, "**So you men could not keep watch with Me for one hour? Keep watching and praying that you may not enter into temptation; the spirit is willing, but the flesh is weak**." He went away again a second time and prayed, saying, "**My Father, if this cannot pass away unless I drink it, Your will be done**." Again He came and found them sleeping, for their eyes were heavy. And He left them again, and went away and prayed a third time, saying the same thing once more. Then He came to the disciples and said to them, "**Are you still sleeping and resting? Behold, the hour is at hand and the Son of Man is being betrayed into the hands of sinners**."* (Matt. 26:36–45; emphasis mine)

In the garden, Jesus, with a soul deeply grieved to the point of death asked Peter, James, and John to stay with Him and keep watch (v. 38).

And after praying earnestly for a reprieve and not getting it, He came back to His disciples, His friends, looking for some companionship; perhaps to share His grief with them and what does He find? Verse 40: they are sleeping and look what He says to them: "***so you men could not keep watch with Me for one hour?***"

Again Christ admonishes them in verse 41: "***Keep watching and praying that you may not enter into temptation…***" Yet again, Christ returns to prayer and seems to come to the understanding that indeed, His mission is to go to the cross. And perhaps looking for companionship once again during these dreadful moments, He returned again to His disciples and found them sleeping.

He found them **without perseverance, without diligence, without intercession**. And once again, He left them to continue in prayer. And when He returned for a third time, He finds the ones in whom the entire Gospel message is entrusted—**sleeping!**

Do We Fall Asleep while We Wait?

Is our perseverance taking a nap? Are we "in the fray", fervently praying, or has *our rationale* decided that God isn't going to answer this prayer? Christ was desperate and relied on His friends. How desperate do we need to be to stay focused on the mission?

Perhaps it's us or perhaps it's the ones we are praying for. They, like Christ, are going through intolerable anguish and pain. They've asked us to pray for them; and as they look around at us hoping to see a lifeline; they find us—sleeping! We've given up. Our prayers aren't being answered and aren't going to be answered. And we are ohhh… so tired!

Do you know what comes to mind? Look at Mark 4:

> *Leaving the crowd, they took Him along with them in the boat, just as He was; and other boats were*

> *with Him. And there arose a fierce gale of wind, and the waves were breaking over the boat so much that the boat was already filling up. Jesus Himself was in the stern, asleep on the cushion; and they woke Him and said to Him, "Teacher, do you not care that we are perishing?"* (Mark 4:36-38)

The irony is pungent.

- The disciples fearful for their lives turn to the one they trust, the one they think just might be God, the one they believe can bring yet another miracle and in their eyes, He doesn't care. He sleeps!
- Christ in the garden, fearful in His humanity of the fate that is coming to Him, turns to His only friends; to the only ones on this earth that He has spent any quality time with, the ones in whom He can confide. And they sleep!

Patience and perseverance are so vital to a fulfilling faith.

A Sunday school class had been writing to foreign missionaries and apparently the teacher had told her class that missionaries were very busy and they should not be discouraged if they didn't get a response to their letter. One letter went like this:

> *Dear Rev Smith, We are praying for you. We are not expecting an answer.*

Without realizing it, the little girl summed up the prayer life of many Christians. Unfortunately, most of us aren't surprised when our prayers are not answered; we're surprised when they are![8]

"*He who watches over you will not slumber*" (Ps. 121:3).

Look at Mark 11:

> *And Jesus answered, saying to them,* ***"Have faith in God. Truly I say to you, whoever says to this mountain 'be taken up and cast into the sea,' and does not doubt in his heart, but believes***

> ***that what he says is going to happen, it will be granted him. Therefore I say to you, all things for which you pray and ask, believe that you have received them, and they will be granted you."*** (Mark 11:22–24; emphasis mine)

This statement is completely parallel to the contents of chapter 13 regarding healing.

We have talked in earlier chapters about your prayers being heard the very moment you utter them, and we've talked about the schemes of the devil and his demonic forces to intercept and try to hijack those petitions. The important words in this passage from Mark are those describing a future event: "**They will be granted you**." We need to understand that life unfolds on God's timetable—not ours. Unlike us, God doesn't have deadlines.

Waiting for answers to prayer tests our resolve, our perseverance and ultimately, sooner or later, our faith. This chapter is titled, "What Matters Most, Your Faith or Your Circumstances?" The correct answer is yes. When you need unmerited favor and turn to God, allowing His grace to bless you and meet your needs, He will see your faith, and you will find His peace.

We all have circumstances in our lives. The question is what do we do with them?

The first thing that we just discussed is to put your faith to work being patient and persevering. Remember that God deals either in the present or in the future. We, for the most part, either deal in the past (as we relive our regrets) or in the present. The lyrics to an old country and western song remind me of how we live in the past. There was a line in there that said, "Looking back is the only thing I have to look forward to." When we deal in the present, it always goes something like this: "Lord, I really need this to happen right away."

God, on the other hand, is mostly looking after your future. So if its yesterday, and He's looking after your future, then today is covered; and if it's today, then He's got tomorrow covered.

"*Then I **will** hear from heaven, **will** forgive their sin and **will** heal their land*" (2 Chron. 7:14). "*It **will** be granted him... and they **will** be granted you*" (Mark 11:22–24; emphasis mine).

The second thing to do is **give God your concerns**.

I think women have an easier time asking for help than men. Women feel more at home, more at ease, sharing with their friends. My wife has two groups of women that she gets together with on a regular basis. She calls them her "girlie-girls". She will tell me that she's having supper with the girlie-girls on Wednesday, and they all meet and catch up with things and who knows what else is discussed? But this is healthy behavior for her. I think men struggle to "download" their concerns and issues with other men. I don't know if it's a macho thing or if it's a learned behavior wherein it has been the men in their lives since childhood that have told them to "suck it up," "be a man," "don't quit," "you can do it," etc., etc., etc. And so they struggle to share.

So why would it be any different "downloading" our problems on God? There's a book or an expression in a book out there that says, "Give your problems to God, He's up all night anyway." Many Christians struggle to trust God to help them. They believe they have salvation, that Christ's their Savior; but getting deeper and understanding God's grace has eluded them, and unfortunately, not a lot of churches are preaching grace.

When Adam and Eve ate of the tree of the knowledge of good and evil, they set off a chain reaction that affected the next six to ten billion people (depending on how long earth will last) who will ever exist on this planet. The chain reaction is called sin. Here we have the very first two people on earth out of billions to follow, and they've already screwed up God's plan for peace and serenity. They know they've sinned because they know they're naked. And how does God react? Genesis 3:21 says that God made garments of skin for them to cover their nakedness. God performed the very first animal sacrifice—the very first death of one of the creatures He created—because He loved Adam and Eve.

If this isn't proof that He loves us, fast forward to the cross where Jesus is brutalized physically and emotionally in order to accept all our sin and sickness. We need to look at the Sunday evening of His resurrection to understand where He's at and what He is doing in *our* lives. Notice the similarities between this Scripture and the issues you may be facing in your life.

"So when it was evening on that day, the first day of the week, and when the doors were shut where the disciples were, for fear of the Jews, Jesus came and stood in their midst and said to them, ***'Peace be with you'*** " (John 20:19).

On this Sunday morning, Jesus had appeared to Mary Magdalene (John 20:15). But now He appears to all the disciples, except Thomas, in the very midst of their gathering, in the very core of their fear. It's important to reflect on several things in this passage because two of them—and hopefully, three—happen to us all the time. First, the doors are locked; second, the disciples are frightened; and third, Jesus comes to them right in the middle of all their anxieties, all of their concerns and fears. How can we relate this verse to our lives and how Christ will react with us?

- **The doors are locked**. How often do we shut out the world, our church, our spouse, and our friends when fears engulf us? We get so fed up with people telling us what to do, how to pray, what scripture to read. We're so very disappointed, so angry that God is nowhere to be found. We just feel defeated and there's no way out. But look what happens in the midst of all of this turmoil: Jesus is there! No one went to the door and let Him in! No one opened the door! They didn't hear anyone knock! So my friends, *when you feel that there is no way out, please remember, God can always get in!* He can go to places in your life, in your body, in your spirit, that no therapist, no physician, no pastor can get to. And once there, He brings "peace".
- **They are afraid**. Macho and bravado only last until that phone call at 2:00 a.m.; until that radiology report; until that pink slip comes. I wish with all my heart that I had trained my mind to relax in the arms of Jesus when bad news hits, but when the nurse called and said to me, "There's a dominant mass in your left lung...," my stom-

ach slid to my feet and this cold, prickly sensation swept over my body. Every single member of my family has died from cancer; what chance did I have?* Yet this is where the disciples and other followers found themselves. Their gentle leader who had healed the sick, ministered for only three and a half years, yet had throngs of well-wishers follow Him, was crucified by the Jewish elite by the hands of the Romans. What chance did *they* have? Their Christ is gone but the soldiers and the "PeRPs"[9] are still there!

- **Christ comes with His peace**. Christ, having just been crucified, jumps right back into the fray. Twice He tells them "***Peace be with you.***" And what Jesus is saying to us by these actions is the same as can be found in Deuteronomy 31:6, "*For the Lord your God is the One who goes with you. He will not fail you or forsake you.*" Also Isaiah 41:10, "*Do not fear, for I am with you; do not anxiously look about you, for I am your God. I will strengthen you, surely I will help you, surely I will uphold you with My righteous right hand.*" Christ is telling us "*don't worry if your faith is small, I will strengthen you, I will strengthen your faith.*"

So here you are, all cooped up hiding from the world; frightened about your circumstances. Is it possible that you won't see Jesus "standing in your midst" because of your emotions? I can assure you that at least once in your life, Christ has appeared in your midst. It could have been a phone call from a friend, or an unexpected job offer. And because you have missed His presence in the past, when times were relatively good, you'll miss Him when times are tough and your emotions are all over the map. Please begin now to build that relationship with Him that will sustain you when your world gets turned upside down.

A short time ago, I was fervently praying for a woman in our church (I'll call her Molly), who had constant, debilitating headaches. She couldn't work; had trouble sleeping, traveling, and so on. All the tests were negative. But life for Molly had become unbearable. Her husband had taken her to emergency one night because the pains were so bad. She was subsequently admitted for observation and testing. When I first met her at the hospital, her face was full of anguish as she suffered the pain of her headaches. I prayed with her that night and promised her I would visit again and would continue in prayer for her.

A few days passed, she was released from the hospital and sent home and as I was making my daily phone call to encourage her, I went into my study and opened my cell phone to dial and realized that I didn't have *one thing* to say to her. Nothing! I was out of ideas, out of platitudes, out of sympathies. You know, as I think about it, I was out of hope. I closed the phone, bowed my head, and said, "*Lord, I'm not making this call until you give me something I can say to her.*" In a few chapters, you will read about Intercessory Prayer and Intercession. I found it to be emotionally violent. Christ found it to be physically and emotionally violent when He interceded for us on the cross, and no, I'm not drawing any parallels. I just want you to think about this story when you get to that chapter. Only then will you know how deeply I was committed to Molly and how frustrated I had become with no apparent answer to my prayers.

I told God (not recommended) that I would give Him fifteen minutes to give me something I could give Molly. Well, I did everything I could to keep my mind blank so that I would hear God when He spoke to me. It seemed like forever. At one point, this thought came into my mind: "*Be Still and Know that I am God*" (Ps. 46:10). I remember thinking, *I know that's me, not you God. I'll wait a few more minutes.*

So at the end of fifteen minutes, discouraged, I called Molly. Her voice exuded her pain. Hearing her made me feel even more depressed. We chatted for a few minutes and then I said to her, "*Molly, I have been praying for you and God told me to give this scripture to you; 'Be Still and Know that I am God.'*" We chatted for a few minutes about what that should look like in her current condition and then we prayed and I hung up.

The next evening, I went to visit her, and she was sitting with a book in her lap. She actually sounded and looked a little better, and

I was thrilled for her. She said that her girlfriend had given this book to her several weeks ago, and it was a series of prayers to be read one day at a time over a period of one hundred or maybe one hundred and one days. The devotional and prayer for that day—the day after I called with God's message for her—was titled *Be Still and Know that I am God.* All I could do was smile, but inside my heart was soaring. **Christ had arrived with His Peace**.

Is it your faith or your circumstances? It can be both. Jesus wept over circumstances, over pain and sorrow, over sadness; but John 11:33 also says He was troubled—troubled about the lack of faith. We have no trouble igniting our faith when life is calm; if only we could structure the same intensity in just praising Him when things are hectic. Let me give you a Scripture that you can trust in: "*Every place on which the sole of your foot treads, I have given you possession*" (Josh. 1:3) and two verses later, "*I will be with you; I will not fail you or forsake you*" (Josh. 1:5)

Something to Think About:

Luke 10 tells the story of Jesus visiting with Mary and Martha. It illustrates our chapter on "Faith and Circumstances".

> *Mary, who was seated at the Lord's feet,* ***listening to His word****. But Martha was distracted with all her preparations; and she came up to Him and said, "Lord, do You not care that my sister has left me to do all the* ***serving*** *alone? Then tell her to help me." But the Lord answered and said to her, "****Martha, Martha, you are worried and bothered about so many things; but only one thing is necessary, for Mary has chosen the good part, which shall not be taken away from her****.'"* (Luke 10:39–42; emphasis mine)

Here's the short and sweet: God is more pleased when you feed from Him than when you serve. God is more pleased when you feed your faith than be busy about your circumstances. Remember chapter 2 where Christ knew when Lazarus became sick. He knows more about your circumstances than you do!

*That "dominant mass" was diagnosed as Valley Fever, a fungal infection common to the deserts of the Southwest. Shortly after treatments began, PT scans showed the "mass" to be shrinking.

7

Accessing and Delivering the Power of the Holy Spirit

The slogan "When You Care Enough to Send the Very Best" was first aired in a radio broadcast in 1944. Independent consumer research has identified this Hallmark slogan time and time again as one of the most believed advertising pieces in the United States.

We're a little like this. Not in everything mind you, but in many cases, we put our best foot forward. We dress up for first dates; we're on our best behavior for job interviews; our Facebook page embellishes things a little bit; and if someone important is coming over, we scrub and clean our homes as if royalty were descending. We employ everything we have in order to be seen in a better light.

The good news for our prayer lives is similar in that we can put our very best weapon into the fray. Christlike power is available to us through the Holy Spirit. If you have had concerns about having a weak prayer life, of being uncomfortable praying in public or just feeling that you don't know how to pray or what to say, this chapter will change your life!

Gordon Lindsay, the founder of Christ for the Nations coined the term, *The Substance of Prayer.* The concept is that our prayers do more than motivate the Father to action, they actually **release the power of the Holy Spirit from us to accomplish things.**

Look what 1 Corinthians 3:16 has to say: "*Do you not know that you are a temple of God and that* ***the Spirit of God dwells in you?***" and in 6:19: "*Or do you not know that* ***your body is a temple of the Holy Spirit who is in you, whom you have from God****, and that you are not your own?*"

Many of us have this image of God being on His throne in heaven and while absolutely correct, that's where they leave the concept. **But He has now also made His throne in our hearts and we are the temple of the Holy Spirit. We are now the "holy of holies", the dwelling place of God upon the earth. When He moves to release power upon the earth, it often comes directly from us where His Spirit dwells.**

What are we expected to do with the power of the Holy Spirit? John 16 is spoken to the disciples by Christ and fully explains the powers that reside in you.

> *But I tell you the truth, it is to your advantage that I go away; for if I do not go away, the Helper will not come to you; but if I go, I will send Him to you. And He, when He comes, will convict the world concerning sin and righteousness and judgment; concerning sin, because they do not believe in Me; and concerning righteousness, because I go to the Father and you no longer see Me; and concerning judgment, because the ruler of this world has been judged. I have many more things to say to you, but you cannot bear them now. But when He, the Spirit of truth comes, He will guide you into all the truth; for He will not speak on His own initiative, but whatever He hears,*

> *He will speak; and He will disclose to you what is to come. He will glorify Me, for He will take of Mine and will disclose it to you. All things that the Father has are Mine; therefore, I said that He takes of Mine and will disclose it to you."* (John 16:7–15)

When we read through the book of John chapters 14, 15, and 16, we find that Christ, knowing that the disciples' world is soon to be turned upside down, promises these things to them:

- a place in heaven,
- an ongoing spiritual relationship with Christ,
- access to Him in prayer,
- the presence of the Holy Spirit,
- the continuance of His mighty works,
- that the Holy Spirit would guide them into all truth (John 16:13),
- That He will return.

These are the same promises that have been given to us; that we can claim because we believe the Scriptures, and we believe we are indwelled by the Holy Spirit. The multiple dimensions of the Holy Spirit are revealed as Spiritual Gifts in 1 Corinthians 12:4–11. We learn that the various gifts of the Holy Spirit are wisdom, knowledge, faith, healing, miracles, and prophecy and so on. Let me assure you that you have been blessed by one of these gifts. Take some time in prayer and ask God what your gift is and how you can use it.

Why are the Spirit's powers released through us? Christ mentioned several things in the Scriptures above. First Corinthians 12:7 adds this: "*But to each one is given the manifestation of the Spirit for the common good.*" Another answer is found in the words of Christ in Matthew 16:18, "*And upon this rock I will build My church; and the gates of Hades will not overpower it.*"

The "rock" that Christ refers to is the one fact that holds all Christianity together: that Jesus Christ is the Son of God, the Savior, the Redeemer, and as He says in John 14:6, "*I am the way, and the truth, and the life; no one comes to the Father but through Me.*" On these facts, Christ will build His church and the Holy Spirit, given to all believers not only helps us to withstand the world and sustain the message, it also allows us to bring His gifts to the world—***for the common good***. It is God's plan to release the powers of the Holy Spirit through us. He has given us the power, the Spirit's gifts, and the protection to get His will done on earth. Never forget that "partnership" thing.

Let me say right now (and we will discover something amazing a little later in the chapter) that we have incredible, untapped power within us, simply because we believe that Jesus Christ is our Lord, and that the Holy Spirit dwells within us. We are asked to use that power to preach the good news to the lost; to bring word of redemption and salvation; to introduce the Savior to a still-dark and unenlightened world; to bring healing, comfort, and love to the unfortunate; or to do ***for the common good***.

The world won't teach us how to do these things even though the human condition yearns to rely on surroundings that we can see, feel, and touch, but with the power of the Holy Spirit, we can do great and mighty things.

- We have the ability to pray in the Spirit. This gives us an incredible pathway straight to God, Himself. Romans 8:26 says, "*In the same way the Spirit also helps our weakness; for we do not know how to pray as we should, but the Spirit Himself intercedes for us with groanings too deep for words.*" The Spirit intercedes directly to God for us!
- Ephesians 6:17 tells us to speak the Word of God as a sword of the Spirit into situations. The sword, which represents God's word (the Bible), is the only offensive weapon that God says we need.
- Matt. 17:20 and Mark 11:23 tell us to declare or command events to occur. They suggest that supernatural things can happen when we employ the Spirit's power. We will see Scripture about this a little later.
- This whole message about having the Holy Spirit within us can be summarized by reading the words of Christ in Mark 16:

> *Go into all the world and preach the gospel to all creation. He who has believed and has been baptized shall be saved; but he who has disbelieved shall be condemned. These signs will accompany those who have believed; in My name they will cast out demons, they will speak with new tongues; they will pick up serpents, and if they drink any deadly poison, it will not hurt them; they will lay hands on the sick, and they will recover. Mark 16:15-18*

Are you ready to be amazed at the power you have been given? Look at John 7:38–39(a): "***He who believes in Me, as the Scripture said, 'From his innermost being will flow rivers of living water.'*** *But this He spoke of the Spirit, whom those who believed in Him were to receive.*"

The *innermost being* in the Greek, is the word "koilia," which literally means "**womb, the soul, the heart, the seat of thought or feeling**." Translating literally, we would say, "**Out of our very essence, our core, our area of compassion, shall flow rivers of living water**."

This suggests that through the Holy Spirit; through us, Christ continues His ministry on earth. This ministry flows from within the deepest, most holy areas of His people, His church. The *innermost being* that Christ addresses, and the Greek first interprets as *womb* infers not only life, but *new life!* Out of wombs come *new life!* It suggests that as we mature, as we allow the Holy Spirit to take control of us, we release fresh wind, fresh spirit, and fresh fire into His world. Like a flower will reproduce from its seeds each spring; we reproduce the ministry of Christ from our seeds, our wombs, as the Holy Spirit works through us.

God's power flows from His people into the world! Anyone can manifest it; missionaries, hospital and nursing home visitors, Sunday school teachers, choir and worship team members. And let's not forget Bible study leaders, prayer chains and Pastors. When we speak, pray, touch or lay hands on the sick, God's power is at work!

And now, the second shock to your system! Let me quote another Scripture to you.

> *Then he showed me a* ***river of the water of life****, clear as crystal,* ***coming from the throne of God and of the Lamb****, in the middle of its street. On either side of the river was the tree of life, bearing twelve kinds of fruit, yielding its fruit every month;* ***and the leaves of the tree were for the healing of the nations.*** (Rev. 22:1–2; emphasis mine)

Please! Don't miss this! This passage speaks of the *river of the water of life* flowing out of the Lamb, out of Jesus, growing and nourishing the trees on either side from which the people of the nations are nourished and made whole. "**River of the water of life**" *is the same Greek translation for* "**rivers of living water**" in John 7!

There is no difference between the river of life flowing out of the Lamb bringing healing and wholeness to the earth, and the rivers of living water that are available to flow from the womb of the Church. Can you see how this relates to the Scripture above, Mark 16:17–18? Go back and read it again.

Do we need any more proof that God wants a partnership with us to bring His ministry to those around us? We are the womb from which His message comes. We are the answer with the power to His proclamation that we just read in Mark 16:15, "*Go into all the world and preach the gospel to all creation.*"

Does any of this give you renewed hope for your prayer life? Does having this kind of power available to you encourage you to pray healing, prosperity, or salvation into situations? When you find people who will bring rivers of living water from the river of life to speak over your needs, over the needs of others and who will bring healing to your circumstances through faith, you will enjoy victorious living.

Jesus wept because He saw the compassion regarding Lazarus that all His disciples and followers would need in order to go forth and take His message to a world that will always be hurting unless they accept Him as their Lord and Savior.

Understanding and Employing the Power

Instincts won't help you. There's nothing in our secular life to tell us about the spiritual powers discussed above. About all we get is the knowledge of receiving the Holy Spirit when we accept Jesus Christ as our Lord. In order to employ these truths, we have to understand that there are varying degrees of power in most spiritual areas. Be very much open to praying for an increase or an abundance in those areas that you feel inadequate in. Let's look at ***love, faith, and power***.

The measurable degrees of love.

"*Greater love has no one than this, that one lay down his life for his friends*" (John 15:13). "*Because lawlessness is increased, most people's love will grow cold*" (Matt. 24:12). "*And this I pray that your love may abound more and more in real knowledge and all discernment*" (Phil. 1:9). So we find greater love, love growing cold and love abounding more and more.

There are measurable levels of faith.

"As God has allotted to each a measure of faith" (Rom. 12:3). We've each been metered out a portion of faith. It's up to us to appropriate the power behind the gift and make it grow. "Because your faith is greatly enlarged" (2 Thess. 1:3). The original "measure" has grown. "That your faith may not fail" (Luke 22:31–32). Apparently, there is a failing faith. I think we've all experienced that. "The apostles said to the Lord, 'Increase our faith'" (Luke 17:5). Just for the asking, faith can be increased.

Let's look at the scripture in Mark 5:30, "*Immediately Jesus, perceiving in Himself that the power proceeding from Him had gone forth, turned around in the crowd and said,* ***'Who touched My garments?'"*** Jesus knew immediately that the healing **power *went out*** of His being, according to the level of the woman's faith. As powerful as that Scripture is, just a few verses later, we are equally stunned at an event in Jesus's hometown of Nazareth.

"*And* ***He could do no miracle there*** *except that He laid His hands on a few sick people and healed them.* ***And He wondered at their unbelief*"** (Mark 6:5–6; also Matt. 13:58). The verse says that because of the unbelief of the Nazarenes, Jesus could not perform a miracle there. The Greek does not say "He chose not to," or "He didn't." It says literally, "He could not." The peoples' level of faith or unbelief had hindered the flow of the power of God. Yet there were some healings; so He apparently could get some power flowing for one thing but not the other. **This implies that differing amounts of faith are required for different things**. Jesus could release enough power to get a few healings, but He couldn't get enough power flowing, because of their unbelief, to work a miracle. It is unbelief and contempt that drive Christ out of the heart, as they did out of his own country. Faith puts all of the power of Almighty God into the hands of men; whereas unbelief appears to tie up even the hands of the Almighty.

For centuries, people believed that Aristotle was right when he said that the heavier an object, the faster it would fall to earth. Aristotle was regarded as the greatest thinker of all time, and surely he would not be wrong. Anyone, of course, could have taken two objects, one heavy and one light, and dropped them from a great height to see whether or not the heavier object landed first. But no one did until nearly two thousand years after Aristotle's death. In 1589, Galileo summoned learned professors to the base of the Leaning Tower of Pisa. Then he went to the top and simultaneously pushed a ten pound and a one pound weight off the structure. Both landed at the same instant. The power of belief was so strong, however, that the professors denied their eyesight. They continued to say Aristotle was right.[10] The power of unbelief, or failing faith, is the flip side of this. Whereas the professors saw something happen and did not believe; we have a tendency to believe something *isn't going to happen because it hasn't yet.* These scenarios usually end with us giving up (there's that persistence thing, again), and then there is neither love nor faith prayed into the situation.

As we Christians struggle to understand and accept that God created man to have a relationship ***and*** a partnership with him, we need to keep in mind the following Scripture from 2 Corinthians 3: "*We are not saying that we can do this work ourselves. It is God who makes us able to do all that we do*" (2 Cor. 3:5, NCV) So when you quit, you are quitting on yourself *and* you are quitting on God.

There are measurable levels of power.

Let's start this study with Matthew 17:

> *When they came to the crowd, a man came up to Jesus, falling on his knees before Him and saying, "Lord, have mercy on my son, for he is a lunatic and is very ill; for he often falls into the fire and often into water. I brought him to Your disciples, and they could not cure him." And Jesus answered and said,* ***"You unbelieving and perverted generation, how long shall I be with you? How long shall I put up with you? Bring him here to Me."*** *And Jesus rebuked him, and the demon came out of him, and the boy was cured at once. Then the disciples came to Jesus privately and said, "Why could we not drive it out?" And He said to them,* ***"Because of the littleness of your faith; for truly I say to you, if you have faith the size of a mustard seed, you will say to this mountain, 'Move from here to there,' and it will move; and nothing will be impossible to you. But this kind does not go out except by prayer and fasting."*** (Matt. 17:14–21; emphasis mine)

The disciples were given power by Jesus and had been casting out demons and healing the sick. But they could not get the job done with the lunatic boy. Jesus, however, had no problem in exorcising the demon. So we see a power gap between the disciples and Jesus. The most obvious conclusion is that there are differing power levels required to get differing acts accomplished.

I believe that this is the reason why prayers take so long to get answered. If a prayer has not been answered, it just may be that there hasn't been enough power released in the spirit to accomplish the task. Most Christians are not aware of this. We pray and sit back and wait for God to answer. And all the time, He's waiting for us to pray more power into the situation. God desperately wants a full partnership with man. He wants us releasing Him to do great things on earth, among His people; but while He waits on us, we get discouraged and ease up on our prayers, and the power fades and we justify life by assuming "it wasn't God's will."

God knows very well that man can grow weary. After all, we rest in our Lord completely out of faith. If it was going to be easy, Jesus wouldn't have talked of mustard seeds, He would have said, "***If you have faith the size of a watermelon…***" But He didn't. Instead He gave us a Scripture in Hebrews 11:1, "*Now faith is the assurance of things hoped for, the conviction of things not seen.*" In other words, "I have certainty that the thoughts and wishes of my mind will become reality, and my beliefs even though unseen, will be manifested."

Look at these two examples in the Old Testament that illustrate the need for praying power into circumstances.

First Kings 17:17–24 speaks of Elijah restoring the life of a woman's son who had died. Verse 21: "*Then he stretched himself upon the child three times, and called to the Lord and said, 'O Lord my God, I pray You, let this child's life return to him.'*" Why did it take three times? Was this man of God not where he needed to be spiritually? Did he not have enough faith? Did he not pray right the first two times? We're not told why but is it possible that he needed to release more and more spiritual power out of his spiritual womb (koila—his innermost being)?

First Kings 18:1–46. In verse 1, God speaks to Elijah, "*Go, show yourself to Ahab and I will send rain on the face of the earth.*" It's important to know that God was very direct: "I will send rain on the face of the earth." God didn't say "I might." He didn't say, "If you pray hard enough." He didn't say, "I'm thinking about it." He just said, "I'm going to do it." It was God's timing, God's idea, God's will. Yet at the end of the chapter, we are told that Elijah labored in prayer diligently **seven times** before clouds appeared and the rain came. **If it was God's will, timing, and idea, why did Elijah have to pray seven times?** Is it possible that God, working that full partnership with man, needed more power released from Elijah's intercession to get the job done?

Why did it take Daniel twenty-one days to get his answer when God sent an angel to tell him his prayer was heard on the very first day? Doesn't God have the power to get an angel through the spiritual warfare? Or was Daniel's faithful praying releasing the power that was needed to break through the demonic opposition? Could God be saying, "I can do this whenever I want, but I want you to feel like part of the solution and that will take a little more time, more perseverance, and more patience? You will never be as mighty as I, but together, you can accomplish great things through faith."

Listen, I'm not for one instant suggesting that God's power is limited. But I am suggesting that God works in accordance with the prayers of His partners—us! It seems reasonable to me that if men's prayers were significant enough to allow the angel to be dispatched, then they would also be the key to breaking through with the message. Although the answer to Daniel's prayer was already granted, who knows what would have happened if Daniel had stopped praying early?

There's a beautiful Scripture that sums up everything I have been saying. Look with me at Ephesians 3: "*Now to Him* (God) *who is able to do far more abundantly beyond all that we ask or think,* ***according to the power that works within us*** (the Holy spirit) *to Him* (God) *be the glory in the church and in Christ Jesus to all generations forever and ever*" (Eph. 3:20-21).

Well, there it is, "**according to the power that works within us…**" After almost seven chapters of study about prayer, it boils down to **the rivers of living water; the river of the water of life flowing out of the Lamb who lives in me—out of my innermost being (koilia)**, going forth and bringing healing to the nations—to the ones I am praying for. The Holy Spirit that resides within every Christian gives us the power to change the world, and all of the circumstances in it, all for God's Glory. Hallelujah!

Ephesians 3:20 also says He has enough power to do more than we can ask or think. So why are we unsatisfied? Why are we deficient? Why are we defeated?

The Power Source is not the problem.

Let's go back to Ephesians 3:20. The word for "far more abundantly beyond" is the same word for the abundant grace of God in Romans 5:20. The Greek word is ***huperperissos***. *Perissos* means superabundant." *Huper* means "beyond" or "more than." Together, they would mean superabundantly with more added to that. That's like saying "more than more than".

The power **source** is not the problem: The rest of Ephesians 3:20 says this, "According to the power that works within us." One bible scholar translates the phrase "In the **measure** of the power, which is operative in us." The word **measure** in the Greek is *kata*. Strong's concordance says not only does this indicate that which is **measured to us**, (Remember Romans 12:3. "*As God has allotted to each a measure of faith.*") but it is also used with the connotation of "distribution".

Putting those translations together, we have, "*He is going to do this superabundantly more than we can ask or think in the measure of the power that is distributed from us.*"

Are you distributing power? Are you distributing the river? It doesn't come from sporadic or casual praying. It must be released from inside of you on a consistent basis. James 5:16 says, "*The effectual fervent prayer of a righteous man availeth much.*" The amplified translation reads, "*The earnest (heartfelt, continued) prayer of a righteous man makes tremendous power available (dynamic in its working).*"

My friends, this has nothing to do with your abilities, the amount of power that has been measured to you, or anything else supernatural. This has everything to do with God. He has given you what you need. We have the same power inside of us that created the world!

Knowing this, if you believe and take into your heart every scripture we have given you in this chapter, you can make a conscious decision to release enormous power into all of your situations. In His full partnership with man, God provided the power; we allow it to be released through our willingness to get involved, as we persist in intercession utilizing our faith to overcome.

Provocative Thoughts. "*Then God said, 'Let* ***Us*** *make man in* ***Our*** *image, according to* ***Our*** *likeness*" (Gen. 1:26). **Us, Our, and Our**. Who's God talking to? Angels? Cherubim? Seraphim? No, no, and no!

When man was created, we have the Father, the Son, and the Holy Spirit gathered together. Man was created with likenesses to the Trinity. (This might be a good time to go back and review chapter 1.)

Man was given the mind of God—able to ponder, formulate, create and embrace, to a certain extent, all the abstract things that we love about God: love, peace, joy, grace, mercy, and so forth.

Man was given the body of Christ destined to go into all the world, to endure, to withstand, and unfortunately, to be battered. It is a house to hold our spirit. It won't be resurrected, it won't prevail. Instead, it will be replaced after the rapture.

Man was given the spirit of Christ—the Holy Spirit. Man's spirit is dead until he accepts Jesus Christ as his Lord and Savior. At that point, the Holy Spirit unites with our spirit and brings us Righteousness, according to Romans 8:10.

We are tripartite! Spirit, Soul, Body! We have been created with elements of the Trinity. The body can do nothing without the mind or soul, and the mind can act independent from the spirit. The mind dwells on worldly things and this affects the body. We must train our mind to dwell on the spirit, on spiritual things, on righteousness. Romans 8:11 tells us that, "*He who raised Christ Jesus from the dead will also* ***give life to your mortal bodies*** *through His Spirit who dwells in you.*"

How is it that you are sick when the Healer lives inside of you?

8

Intercessory Prayer, Just the Beginning

When Christians venture into intercession and intercessory prayer they are often surprised at just how intense the battle can be. They don't realize the commitment that awaits them, the sense of failure that can consume them, and most of all, how quickly they will run out of their own resources. Intercessory prayer can **weaken us** like no other; it can be **discouraging**, and it will **demand that we turn to God** as we search for things to say; it **changes *our* life** as we take on parts of the life of the one being prayed for; it **consumes us** with concern, which **leads us to confront God** like we've never done before. It **produces challenges and trials** and **brings us face to face with our faith.**

One of the reasons I spent so much time on the **"living streams"** concept and the study we just finished on understanding and accessing the power that is available through us was to prepare you for this chapter on **intercessory prayer** and to equip you to guard against all the pitfalls that lie in waiting when you intercede. And so, despite all the drawbacks or negatives I listed in the previous paragraph, let me say this: intercessory prayer can be the most **rewarding, satisfying, uplifting, fulfilling, and inspirational effort we can put forth as human partners with God**.

My advice to those of you eager to intercede for others who are struggling is to understand and assess what level of involvement you feel the most comfortable with. The truth is, irrespective of how much time the intercessor has for this ministry, he or she will run out of emotional resources long before they run out of time. The most perfect intercessor we have ever known is our Lord Jesus. The seventeenth chapter of the Gospel of John has to be the words of Christ with perhaps John's memory enhanced by the Holy Spirit, because it is very much a testimony of One who lived it, by One who has been there, by One who loved it so deeply. We'll look at it a little later.

Intercession will change your life. Intercession will exhaust you, exhilarate you, and expand your faith and your walk with God. Here are four levels of involvement that may help you decide where you want to be. You may know of more, but these are the four where I have found most people belong. I have listed them by number of participants, from the greatest to the least.

1. **Prayers and Greetings**. These are the people who perhaps belong to a deacon group who meet regularly to pray over a list that has been compiled of church members needing prayer. They participate in prayer chains and spend regular, daily times praying for the needs of others. Often, this ministry will send cards with greetings of encouragement, sorrow or get well. This is a very important group in the church.
2. **Prayers, Greetings, and Visits**. All of the above except that some of the people will want to visit with the individuals requesting prayer to show that the church cares, that they are not alone in their need. Oftentimes, these caring people will spend time with the sick and will do a Bible study or play cards or just encourage conversation. These loving people help those in need to pass long, lonely hours with a caring person.

3. **The Identity Shift Gang**. We will get into more detail in the following pages of this study, but for now, their characteristics include: Visiting often, bringing prayers, and expectations of healing; taking on the hurts and concerns of the needy (which involves actually living their lives parallel to the one hurting), praying night and day, asking for God's guidance; making this ministry a priority in their life; and overall, being so involved that their spirit groans as they appeal to God for a restoration.
4. **Identity Shift Ministry**. These people have been at level three and wish to expand their influence by carefully selecting others to join them in this delicate yet powerful ministry. The newcomers *shadow* the originals as they learn what to say, what to do, how to pray, how to be immersed, how to win the affection and trust of the needy. They learn how to be forcefully gentle, ensuring that those just looking for pity are not only listened to but also lifted up by the hope and revelation of Scripture.

Here's a simple "*rule of thumb*" for you if you are planning on praying for another. Let's say you get a prayer request from the prayer chain at your church to pray for "Robert", who is going in for surgery tomorrow. Pray as if you were Robert's son or daughter; his wife, father, or mother. Treat Robert as if he is the closest, dearest thing on earth to you. In doing this, in pursuing this identity change, you will begin to see and feel, not only what Robert is going through but what intercession is all about.

Knowing the power you are going to need in your efforts at intercession, I want to review a Scripture we looked at in the last chapter, Ephesians 3:20: "*Now to Him who is able to do far more abundantly beyond all that we ask or think,* ***according to the power that works within us****, to Him be the glory in the church and in Christ Jesus to all generations forever and ever*" (emphasis added).

It's worth remembering from chapter 7 how we looked at other scholars' interpretive translations that would read like this: "*He is going to do this superabundantly more than we can ask or think in the* ***measure of the power that is distributed from us.***"

It is important that we are aware of the power available to us if we are to enter into intercession and prayer. We are required to have **concern and bring comfort** to others **just as Christ has concern and brings comfort to us.** Intercession and empathy (not sympathy) in combination form the word "interpathy". Here it is, biblically.

> *Blessed be the God and Father of our Lord Jesus Christ, the Father of mercies and God of all* ***comfort****, who* ***comforts*** *us in all our affliction so that we will be able to* ***comfort*** *those who are in any affliction with the* ***comfort*** *with which we ourselves are* ***comforted*** *by God. For just as the sufferings of Christ are ours in abundance, so also our* ***comfort*** *is abundant through Christ. But if we are afflicted, it is for your* ***comfort*** *and salvation; or if we are* ***comforted****, it is for your* ***comfort****, which is effective in the patient enduring of the same sufferings which we also suffer; and our hope for you is firmly grounded, knowing that as you are sharers of our sufferings, so also you are sharers of our* ***comfort****. For we do not want you to be unaware, brethren, of our affliction which came to us in Asia, that we were burdened excessively, beyond our strength, so that we despaired even of life; indeed, we had the sentence of death within ourselves so that we would not trust in ourselves, but in God who raises the dead; who delivered us from so great a peril of death, and will deliver us, He on whom we have set our hope. And He will yet deliver us. You also joining in helping us through your prayers, so that thanks may be given by many persons on our behalf for the favor bestowed on us through the prayers of many."* (2 Cor. 1:3–11; emphasis mine)

Sorry to put you through such a long Scripture. At the same time, I hope you noticed the repetition of being comforted and comforting others. In fact, God often uses people (there's that partnership thing again) to minister to others based on the experiences they have had in their lives. Oswald Chambers (1874–1917), a prominent Christian minister and writer best known as the author of the widely read devotional

My Utmost for His Highest wrote: "*If you are going to be used by God, he will take you through a multitude of experiences that are not meant for you at all; they are meant to make you useful in his hands.*"

Who wouldn't want to be tapped on the shoulder by God and hear the words, "I need you?" Well, it's not quite that obvious; it's more like something comes across your path that touches your heart and you jump into the gap and God uses you. The failure occurs when you don't recognize the opportunities God drops into your lap. The motto for being ready when God calls is this: "***Don't hold on to your blessings so tightly that you don't recognize when God asks if He can use them from time to time.***"

Verse 2 tells us that God is the source of grace and peace; then of mercies and all comfort in verse 3. What does God do with these life-saving, life-changing blessings? Verse 4 tells us that He "*comforts us in **all** our affliction so that we will be able to comfort those who are in **any** affliction with the comfort with which we ourselves are comforted by God.*"

Just prior to being seized in the garden of Gethsemane, Christ is engaging in what we call the Last Supper with the disciples. They are squabbling over who will be recognized as greatest and least in the kingdom. Christ, knowing the persecution that awaits them, says to Peter in Luke 22: "*Simon, Simon, behold, Satan has demanded permission to sift you like wheat; but I have prayed for you, that your faith may not fail; and you, when once you have turned again, strengthen your brothers*" (Luke 22:31–32).

There is so much in these two verses; it is difficult to know where to begin. First, the act of "sifting" or threshing wheat is a violent action that strips the kernel from the stalk. Here's an online description of how to do it by hand: "*Hold the bundle in one hand inside a large trash can.* ***Vigorously beat*** *the bundle against the inside of the trash can to separate the wheat kernels from the stalks.* ***Continue beating the wheat****—threshing it—until no more kernels remain on the stalks. Then* ***throw away*** *the stalks that are left in either the trash or the compost pile."*

This is what Satan wanted to do to Peter; this is what Satan wants to do to you, to your family, to those you are praying for. And this is what Satan very nearly accomplished in Peter. Before the rooster crowed three times, Peter's courage and loyalty ***failed*** and his faith very nearly failed, saved only by Christ's prayers.

Verse 32 reveals what we have been looking at in 2nd Corinthians, above; Christ tells Peter, when you recover from all of this shock and persecution, strengthen your brothers who will also be weakened. Use all of your experiences, your victories, your blessings to bring comfort to others. Folks, are you starting to see how this partnership "thing" works? If Christ is instructing Peter to have interpathy and intercede rather than just leave it up to the Holy Spirit, or to God, then surely He wants us to do the same.

Christ also prays for *us*. He intercedes for His children. The same children who haven't quite gotten their mind around grace and definitely haven't understood the finished works of healing, broken-heartedness, and reconciliation that Christ completed on the cross. He shows Himself to be a tender, merciful, understanding, consoling, and comforting God, lifting us up above all our tribulations and anxieties. And what are we to do with all this lavished love? Just like God, we are to intercede, acting as true partners would, by bringing similar consolation and gifts to others.

Imagine for a moment, a virtuoso child prodigy playing piano or violin from a young age. Day after day, month after month, the child studies, practices, writes opus after opus and becomes—well, he becomes nothing; he's unknown; no one has heard him play; no one has heard his music. He has never left his home; never entered a concert hall, never played to an audience. His gifts have never been used to inspire or impact others. How similar we are, who have been so blessed, but don't rush to bless others.

Paul concludes this passage of intercession in 2 Corinthians by acknowledging in verses 8–10 that their journey brought them so close to death that they despaired of living and turned to God to retain their lives because He had the ability to do that, having raised others *from* the dead. But Paul then gives us the picture of the prize in verse 11 when we intercede; "*You also joining in helping us through your prayers, so that thanks may be given by many persons on our behalf for the favor bestowed on us through the prayers of many.*"

The prayers of many intercede and obtain God's blessing; and we feel that thankfulness that comes afterwards and know it is the acknowledgement of God's grace and mercy. The circle is complete.

Are there any ways we could be more like Christ than when we are praying for others? **God interceded** into humanity when He sent Jesus; **Jesus intercedes** for mankind, **the Holy Spirit is interceding** continuously; so why shouldn't we **intercede?**

I learned in my own periods of intercession that there's no such thing as quit. Quit doesn't work; it leaves you unfulfilled; it leaves you feeling hollow and shallow. If you want to quit, don't start. It's better not to begin than to quit. One of the most beautiful *non sequiturs* in the Bible occurs in the Gospel of Luke 11:

> *It happened that while Jesus was praying in a certain place, after He had finished, one of His disciples said to Him, "Lord, teach us to pray just as John also taught his disciples." And He said to them,* ***"When you pray, say: 'Father, hallowed be Your name. Your kingdom come. Give us each day our daily bread. (4) And forgive us our sins, for we ourselves also forgive everyone who is indebted to us. And lead us not into temptation.'"*** (Luke 11:1–4; emphasis mine)

Now without exception, other than some minor variations, we all recognize this as "The Lord's Prayer." The disciples have asked Christ to teach them how to pray; and He does; but it is what He teaches them *in the very next few verses* that fascinates me.

> *Then He said to them, "**Suppose one of you has a friend, and goes to him at midnight and says to him, 'Friend, lend me three loaves; for a friend of mine has come to me from a journey, and I have nothing to set before him'; and from inside he answers and says, 'Do not bother me; the door has already been shut and my children and I are in bed; I cannot get up and give you anything.' I tell you, even though he will not get up and give him anything because he is his friend, yet because of his persistence he will get up and give him as much as he needs.**"* (Luke 11:5–8; emphasis mine)

Friends, nothing in the Bible is coincidental or inconsequential. Things are laid out in the right wording and the right sequencing for one purpose—to give the reader a complete understanding, without any doubt. Christ knew that Christians would pray. We've been praying the Lord's Prayer for two thousand years. But Christ also knew that answers to prayer may take some time, as we've already seen. **He teaches us how to pray, then He teaches us to be determined, persistent, relentless, and even pushy in our prayers**.

The times were very hard for the people of Israel. There was the Roman occupation, which means that there were foreign soldiers in control of the country. They stole, raped, and terrorized the people. The rulers were Roman-appointed, which meant that you did not get justice because the rulers didn't care about you or your country. Taxes were very high, and the collectors were brutal about collecting them. Homes were small and generally made of sand, which would retain moisture and coldness. One can only imagine in this life of poverty and suppression that these small homes likely had only one bedroom, and that entire families slept together to keep warm. Verse 7 says, "*My children and I are in bed.*" Getting up to satisfy the neighbor would disrupt everyone and bring renewed coldness into the sleeping area. Not even being a ***friend,*** (The **Hebrew, *Ahab***, can also be used for the love between parents and their children. A special use of this word relates to an especially close attachment of friends, as seen in Leviticus 19:34 or Deuteronomy 10:19, "*Thou shalt love thy neighbor as thyself.*")[11] would get this neighbor up. But according to verse 8, *persistence* got him up.

A few verses later in Luke 18, Christ again encourages determination:

> *Now He was telling them a parable to show that at all times they ought to* ***pray and not to lose heart,*** *saying,* ***"In a certain city there was a judge who did not fear God and did not respect man. There was a widow in that city, and she kept coming to him, saying, 'Give me legal protection from my opponent.' For a while he was unwilling; but afterward he said to himself, 'Even though I do not fear God nor respect man, yet because this widow bothers me, I will give her legal protection, otherwise by continually coming she will wear me out.' And the Lord said, "Hear what the unrighteous judge said; Now, will not God bring about justice for His elect who cry to Him day and night, and will He delay long over them? I tell you that He will bring about justice for them quickly. However, when the Son of Man comes, will He find faith on the earth?"*** (Luke 18:1–8; emphasis mine)

This statement in itself is a telling testimony to persistence but look below the surface at the real meaning: "***she will wear me out***;" i.e., stun me. This is a metaphor taken from boxers, who bruise each other, and by beating each other about the face, blacken the eyes. It is used again in 1 Corinthians 9:27. Now look what Jesus says in verses 6–8. We also need to be tough, bold, and persistent, to cry out day and night. In the vernacular, we need to get in God's face (respectfully) to show Him how committed we are. And if not, Jesus wonders if He will find faith on the earth when He returns. In other words, if you persist and succeed, your faith will be strengthened; but if your prayers are half-hearted and you give up quickly, your faith will fail, and Christ will not find people of faith when He returns. Instead He will find disheartened quitters.

Abraham gets in God's face (*respectfully, as I mentioned above*) when God shares His plan to destroy Sodom and Gomorrah for their unrighteousness or as God puts it in Genesis 18:20, "*And their sin is exceedingly grave.*" I suggest that you read Genesis 18:16–33. I am only going to show the verses on persistence and God's response to Abraham.

Abraham - 18:23–25: Abraham challenges God to spare the city if He finds **fifty** righteous people. Listen to His boldness in verse 25: "*Far be it from You to do such a thing, to slay the righteous with the wicked, so that the righteous and the wicked are treated alike.*" Then Abraham gets a little angry with God: "*Far be it from You! Shall not the Judge of all the earth deal justly?*" **God - 18:26**: "*If I find in Sodom **fifty** righteous within the city, then I will spare the whole place on their account.*"

Abraham - 18:27–28: Abraham apologizes to the Lord and asks if the fifty are five short, would God destroy the whole city because of five? **God - 18:28**: "*I will not destroy it if I find forty-five there.*"

Abraham - 18:29: Abraham persists and asks, what about forty? **God - 18:29**: "I *will not do it on account of the forty.*"

Abraham - 18:30: Abraham asks that God not be angry with him and asks about thirty. **God - 18:30**: "*I will not do it if I find thirty there.*"

Abraham - 18:31: Abraham asks what will happen if the Lord finds twenty righteous people there. **God - 18:31**: "*I will not destroy it on account of the twenty.*"

Abraham - 18:32: Abraham asks that the Lord not be angry with him saying he will speak just this once. (Really? That's comical because this is the **sixth time** he has petitioned God. Remember this is on the topic of persistence!) "*Suppose ten are found there?*" **God - 18:32**: "*I will not destroy it on account of the ten.*"

The Invariable Principle of Justice

Many people have great intentions in their hearts but they feel a lack of confidence when approaching God with their prayers. **Abraham gives us a vital strategy or line of attack**. In verse 23, Abraham asks, "*Will You indeed sweep away the righteous with the wicked?*" Abraham lays down this ***invariable principle of justice***; that the righteous shall not be punished for the crimes of the wicked. This is the foundation of his supplications. Who among us can pray with any hope of success if we can't assign a reason to God and His conscience for the petitions being offered? The great sacrifice offered by Christ is an infinite reason why a penitent sinner should expect to find the mercy for which he pleads.

We have to expect, because of the precise accuracy of the Bible, that it was God's will to destroy Sodom and Gomorrah and when Abraham interceded for saving it if fifty righteous people were found, then that became God's threshold. Think back to our chapter on "God's Sovereignty, God's Will… So Why Bother?" I made the statement that God's will is always sovereign, but I cautioned the petitioner to always anticipate that His grace and His mercy could replace that will any time God desired.

Here's another point that is clearly made in these scriptures. **Please don't miss this**. Look what happens in verse 33: "*As soon as He had finished speaking to Abraham the Lord departed, and Abraham returned to his place.*" Abraham draws near to God by affection and faith, and in the most devout and humble manner makes intercession through prayer and supplication; and every petition is answered on the spot. **God only ceases His promise to show mercy when Abraham ceases to intercede! Abraham stops interceding, God departs.** That speaks volumes for the case of ***persistence!***

The lesson from these Scriptures is to be persistent with God. Somehow we don't expect someone to challenge God that harshly; but perhaps that's what it takes. Ask for big things, ask often and be like Jacob in Genesis 32:24 who wrestled with God all night to obtain his blessing. In fact, God changed Jacob's name after this to

Israel, which means *"he fights or **persists** with God"* *(in prevailing prayer)* **Become an "Israel"!**

Intercession is all about accepting the assignment!

There are likely only a handful of quarterbacks in the NFL (past and present) who thrive on leading their team to victory in the last two minutes of the game—a situation known as the "two-minute drill". In these times, there is no one else to turn to; not the head coach, not the offensive coordinator, not the backup QB. In fact, it would have much better if their team had scored earlier and more often so that they were leading the game as it wound down. But that didn't happen and here they are with the outcome resting on their shoulders. These are the players who *want* the ball, *want* the situation. These guys flourish in these conditions. Not all do, even though all try their best. There's just some driving force in these others that sets them apart and brings fulfillment.

In life away from sports, the same thing happens to us. Situations present themselves that require going into a "two minute drill" frenzy. Desperate situations require desperate responses.

Moses didn't want the "Exodus" assignment, but he took it. It's all recorded in Exodus 32:1–14. We know Moses to be weak with the Lord. He doesn't feel capable of leading his people out of Egypt. He begs God to get someone else, even volunteers his brother Aaron! Moses stutters in his speech, but he becomes a bold and audacious intercessor in this scene. Here's a little background:

From the very beginning of the exodus from Egypt, the Hebrew people have complained: the water is bitter, there *is* no water, there's no food, and they want to return to bondage in Egypt rather than proceed to the promised land. In short, it's not that they don't trust God, rather they don't know God! They have been displaced from their homeland for more than four hundred years! It's very likely they have picked up many of the customs (and gods) of their captors, the Egyptians, during their more than two hundred years there, and despite all they have seen God do, when things aren't going well, they don't complain to God, they complain to Moses! It's important to understand that they have been under Grace since leaving Egypt—not one person has died. But that is soon going to change. After waiting forty days for Moses to come down from Mount Sinai with the Ten Commandments, the people break their covenant with God (see Exodus 24:7). They melt their gold jewelry, which was likely taken from the Egyptians before they left, and Aaron, Moses's brother, fashions it into a molten calf—a throwback to their life in Egypt.

"*So the next day they (the Israelites) rose early and offered burnt offerings; and brought peace offerings; and the people sat down to eat and to drink, and rose up to play*" (Exod. 32:6).

The Hebrew for the word "play" is **naga** (naw-gah) and likely refers to sexual contact among the people, in light of the drinking and possible nakedness. Some scholars suggest that this feast became a drunken sex orgy. In any event, it greatly offended God. Look what He says to Moses in the following verses:

> *Go down at once, for your people, whom you brought up from the land of Egypt, have corrupted themselves. They have quickly turned aside from the way which I commanded them. They have made for themselves a molten calf, and have worshiped it and have sacrificed to it and said, "This is your God, O Israel, who brought you up from the land of Egypt!" The Lord said to Moses, "I have seen this people, and behold, they are an obstinate people. Now let Me alone, that My anger may burn against them and that I may* ***destroy them.***" (Exod. 32:7–10; emphasis mine)

Clearly, God's patience is exhausted. The Israelites have been complaining the whole time. And now, they have fashioned a golden idol in the form of a calf, claiming this idol brought them out of Egypt! God is ready to terminate their existence! But Moses intercedes for them in verses 12–14: "*Why should the Egyptians speak, saying, 'With evil intent He brought them out to kill them in the mountains and to destroy them from the face of the earth'? Turn from Your burning anger and change Your mind about doing harm to Your people."*

Moses, just as we saw Abraham do back, lays out this ***invariable principle of justice*** whereby God can't proceed because it violates several promises: (a) these are the chosen people. You can't destroy them. (b) Neither God's name nor His purposes can ever be brought into question. God's intent was to bring the Israelites out safely—not to do something that the Egyptians could laugh at. (c) The Abrahamic covenant promising future generations through Abraham's seed would be broken if the Israelites were destroyed. Moses continues:

> *Remember Abraham, Isaac and Israel, Your servants to whom You swore by Yourself, and said to them, "I will multiply your descendants as the stars of the heavens, and all this land of which I have spoken I will give to your descendants, and they shall inherit it forever." So the Lord* ***changed His mind*** *about the harm which He said He would do to His people.*

Moses accepted the assignment and boldly executed the two-minute drill. The entire nation of Israel was at risk. It was a desperate situation and Moses offered his desperate response.

Both Abraham and Moses were firm with God. Situations were desperate and desperate men stood up to intercede. They didn't pause to consider what God's will might be. They thought about doing right for the righteous and doing what was right to ensure God's glory. Because of their persistence, they prevailed with God, and you need to know that you can too!

In your intercessions, remember these few points: battles and victories are not assignments for the reluctant; prevailing against the enemy will never be known to the uncommitted. If you don't want to be involved, you will always find an excuse, while those with an understanding of the need will always find a way. This world is full of people with horrible and appalling situations that are desperate; unfortunately, many Christians are not.

As you deepen your intercession, look for examples of the ***invariable principle of justice*** that I spoke of above.

God loves intercessors*. Adam was God's first intercessor. God loved and protected him and Eve even after sinning. The Bible is replete with intercessors: Abraham, Isaac, and Jacob, All of the prophets, Mary, Paul, James, Peter, John, and so on. The greatest intercessor of course was, and is Jesus Christ.*

If you are contemplating coming alongside someone, jumping into the fray, interceding in prayer; ask God at what level He would like you to start. Continually pray for wisdom and guidance.

9

Intercession: Godly Resources, Identity Shifts, and Violence

Intercession Requires Godly Resources

You may remember my story in chapter 6 about Molly, the lady with the severe headaches and how I reached a point whereby I had picked up the phone to call her and realized that I had absolutely nothing to say to her. I turned to God that night, and He showed me that He was using *me* to deliver healing to her. Those were times when the streams of living water were indeed flowing, bringing healing. All I had to provide was the willingness, the persistence, the identity shift and to accept the assignment. Going through it, I didn't see it; I could have easily missed it, became discouraged and moved on.

You will reach a similar point in your intercessions. There will be periods where nothing seems to be happening. Times when situations don't improve. In fact, they may get worse; despair sets in, and you have nothing to offer. You will be tempted to quit, to pull back. This chapter and the next one should convince you that God hasn't quit, and neither should you.

In those times where everything seems to be static or motionless, I want you to remember one very important thing: You are never praying alone—there is someone else praying with you; the Holy Spirit. Of course, intercessory prayer must start with you. Don't depend on, relax in the knowledge of, or trust the actions of any others who may be stepping up alongside of you. It's great to know that others are there; but God wants *you* to make the investment also. God wants *you* to stretch *your* faith; to put something on the line. Otherwise, it's too cheap to be real. When God's love is working in your life, your love will work in the lives of others. Don't be tepid; be persistent and stubborn. God doesn't mind; God loves an enthusiastic heart.

It is in these times of stillness and inactivity when we realize that our inadequate resources have to make us desperate, not reluctant. I'm reminded of a journey that Christ was on when He came to the city of Sychar in Samaria. Even though Jews in that time refused to deal with the Samaritans because they were of mixed Gentile blood and therefore unclean, Christ rested from His journey by sitting near Jacob's Well. When He asked a Samaritan woman who was there to draw water, for a drink, she, after chiding Him for doing so, said to Our Lord in John 4:11, "*Sir, You have nothing to draw with and the well is deep.*"

This just smacks of Satan: "*You aren't good enough, bright enough or determined enough to accomplish that! You have nothing! No character, no morality and no energy! And besides, this task is too big for you! You're in way over your head!*"

Well (no pun intended) you're right about that, Satan. But it's not my power, it's the Holy Spirit's power; it's the streams of living water that provide. These *aren't* my works, they're the works of God; and as for the task of being too big for me, I agree; but there's no task too big for God! "*Greater is He who is in you than he (Satan) who is in the world*" (1 John 4:4).

This is what the neighbor said to his friend in Luke 11:6: "*For a friend of mine has come to me from a journey, and* ***I have nothing to set before him.***" (I have nothing to draw with) And the friend answered in verse 7, *"Do not bother me; the door has already been shut and my children and I are in bed; I cannot get up and give you anything.*" (So many things will have to happen for me to get out of bed. I'm a long way from helping you) Translation: "And the well is deep." (The water is out of reach for you.)

When circumstances like these beset you, and they will early on, it's best to begin any intercession with prayer and ask God to give you all of the resources you will need. Christ, through the Holy Spirit is telling us, "I am your source. I will supply the living water for those you are praying for." Lean on Me.

It was Christmas morning, 2011. I had been praying with a wonderful couple in our church over their grown son whose health was critical due to heart issues. My own extended family was due to arrive around ten that morning to celebrate Christmas, so I got up early, showered, and left for the hospital to be with this family. When I arrived at Brent's room, I noticed that the bed was made up, the get well cards and balloons were gone and he was nowhere in sight. My heart sank. I went to the nurses' station on the floor and asked where he was. "He's gone!" was the reply. "Gone? What do you mean '*gone*? Gone…" (I pointed toward heaven, asking or gesturing the question, "Did he die?") "They took him to Mayo early this morning."

I spent until about noon with the family at Mayo, praying and encouraging them before I left for home. The next day, I returned and we all prayed again. It was at about the time that I was getting into my truck in the parking lot ready to leave that Brent passed away.

I had dreamed that previous night that God had lifted Brent out of his bed, out and away from all the negativity, all the unbelief that other family members were openly displaying, healed him and laid him back in that hospital room bed. Excitedly, I had shared with the parents this news. I was devastated later in the day to learn that he was deceased.

I spent a long time afterwards, pondering my intercession, my encouragements, my time with the family, and my dream; I came to this conclusion: Intercession and prayer aren't just about answers, or healing; there's so much more. It's about family; it's about experiencing what they are going through; living those hours in their skin, allowing them to lean on you, to use *your* strength; it's about faith, where you are now and where God wants you to be; it's about getting into a deeper relationship with the Almighty whereby you are the clay in the Potter's hands, allowing Him to shape you, and them. It's about learning to be a weapon in God's arsenal—not just for now, but for things that will surface in the future. It's about using all of the resources that God shares with you, knowing He won't ask you to give them back; knowing that He has opened His arms and allowed you and others to share in His deliverance.

Two years later, this mom and dad who were in their late seventies, perhaps early eighties, were in a head-on collision and rushed to emergency. She had suffered a ruptured spleen, broken rib, and facial injuries; he, broken ribs and a broken femur. When I arrived and was allowed to see them, the mom looked at me and said, "You taught me so much when Brent was in hospital. I'll be just fine, don't worry."

Who among us have sufficient resources of our own for these needs? Without turning to God and asking for the insight, the compassion, the encouragement and the faith to engage, we may forever be intimidated and simply watch from the sidelines without ever entering the fray, without ever standing in the gap, without ever shedding our comfort zones.

I can't tell you how many times when I have been praying for others that I have been lost for ideas, lost for words; despite all of this power inside of me, I found myself *with nothing to set before them.* Had I not asked for Godly resources, I would have failed. He gave me something "to draw with" and made "the well" a little less deep.

Intercession Requires an Identity Shift

Passionate petitioners, sensing the urgency of desperate needs, will intercede on behalf of the afflicted. God, when He became humanity was a passionate petitioner who, sensing the urgency of our desperation, sent His Intercessor—Jesus Christ. Before we look at this divine intercession, let's examine some others from our Bible.

Look again at the passage in Exodus that we studied in the last chapter. It is now the next day and Moses has returned up the mountain to God, *"But now, if You will, forgive their sin - and if not, **please blot me out from Your book which You have written!**"* (Exod. 32:32; emphasis mine). Moses identified himself with his people. Without their forgiveness, Moses didn't want his salvation either. **Notice the hyphen!** Moses didn't hesitate to attach his deliverance to his peoples' forgiveness. Is there any greater human intercession? Thirteen verses earlier (32:19), Moses was so enraged at the people and their behavior that he threw the tablets that the Lord had prepared down to the ground and smashed them into pieces! His identity shift was complete by the time he had climbed back up the mountain where God rewrote the stone tablets.

Another identity shift occurs in Romans 9: "*I am telling the truth in Christ, I am not lying, my conscience testifies with me in the Holy Spirit, that I have great sorrow and unceasing grief in my heart. **For I could wish that I myself were accursed, separated from Christ for the sake of my brethren, my kinsmen according to the flesh***" (Rom. 9:1–3). Like Moses, Paul's burden for his brethren was so great and overwhelming, he was willing to not only identify himself with them but to stand shoulder to shoulder with them as their souls marched toward hell. That is intercession. **The preeminent requirement for intercession is the willingness to identify with the one in need, and to submit your readiness to take his or her burden**.

Dear friends, I don't want to discourage any of you from interceding; In the first place, God didn't create you to stand prayer-less when there's great need. And second, everyone is an intercessor to some degree. I am only trying to point out to you that intercession needs to be a full-on commitment. At this point, as you ponder intercession, you may be wondering what the differences are between intercessory prayer and normal every day prayer.

- **Intercessory prayer is more hands-on than "casual" prayer**. *Casual prayers* might be any prayer said and left alone such as praying at the beginning of the church service for general blessings, or "Lord I pray that I will get that promotion;" "Lord, bless this food," etc. *Intercessory prayers* involve more of a continuing mission, an identification with the sufferer; they are more one-on-one with the sufferer and the family.
- **The Intercessor must get quiet before God to gain insight and knowledge about God's desire for the sufferer**. It would be like going into a new job and not asking what they expected you to do.
- **The Intercessor must be invested in the sufferer's needs**: things like their domestic situation; where is the family, spiritually; will visitation stave off loneliness and aloneness; is there evidence that the family members are wearing down as caregivers?
- **The Intercessor must deliver the message of Psalm 46:10 "Cease striving and know that I am God."** People believe with all of their heart that no matter how bad things get, they can pull it out. They believe the world revolves around them. God searches for people who believe the world revolves around Him.
- **Deliverance. What is it and how does it pertain to the sufferer and to the Intercessor?** The Israelites despite so many appearances and miracles from God desperately wanted to return to Egypt. God wanted to deliver them to the promised land. Our struggles may have God sharpening, refining us; creating perseverance and hope.
- **Who should be an Intercessor?** Those that believe they can access the power and blessings from the Holy Spirit to bring about healing. Those who are willing to take God at His word when He tells us so many times; "You have not because you ask not." "You have not because you

didn't ask enough…" "You have not because I didn't see the intensity in your heart…" "You have not because you didn't make this a priority."

- **Does intercessory prayer always result in healing?** Sometimes healing comes in ways no one expected and great things are accomplished in the kingdom.
- **What are some of the qualities or weapons in the Intercessors' arsenal?** Words of encouragement, of hope with appropriate Scripture. Those willing to be modern-day Jacobs and "wrestle with God". This needs absolute commitment and compassion 24/7. Seeking information and guidance from God.
- **All-out intercession has to be limited**. No matter how big your heart is, you will not have the time, energy or resources to take on multiple intercessions at the great depths we are talking about. This does not mean you can't go name by name down the church prayer list and pray for people. It means you can't plan on visiting every one of those names; you can't plan to get to know every family need; and you can't plan to deeply identify as outlined above, with every one of those names. You have to let God guide your choices. Allow Him to lay on your heart two or three people that you can intercede for.

One of the greatest intercessory prayers ever given is the one Christ said for His disciples and for us just hours before He was seized in the garden. It occurred just before the Feast of the Passover and concludes a sermon by Christ that starts in the book of John 13:13. Let's look at the prayer in John 17. First, a quick framework that can shape our study:

Verse 1. Christ prays that the Father will be glorified after He Himself receives glory from God.

Verses 2–3. Christ makes two things clear: that He alone can grant eternal life; and that eternal life consists of *knowing* God and *knowing* (in the sense of believing in) Jesus Christ.

Verses 4–8. Christ has glorified His Father by doing what God had willed on earth and then by revealing His Father to His disciples.

Verses 9–16. Christ prays specifically for the disciples only. He desires that they be unified in their beliefs and that God would keep them from Satan.

Verses 17–19. Christ asks God to set these disciples apart for His use and for His Holy purposes.

Verses 20–26. Christ then expands His prayer for all who would believe in God and His Son by hearing the gospel; that they would all be brought into a common understanding resulting eventually in their eternal salvation and glory.

Let's close in on some particular passages to fully see Christ's intercession for His disciples. Remember that Christ knows what difficulties lie ahead. While we intercede during a crisis, Christ is interceding before the crisis hits.

"*I ask on their behalf; I do not ask on behalf of the world, but of those whom You have given Me; for they are yours*" (John 17:9). Christ's whole mind and body is focused on equipping those whose responsibility will be to take the gospel to the world. The hidden subtlety in not praying for the rebellious Jews at this time, (the world) lies in Christ's knowledge that God's judgment on them is still to come.

"*And all things that are Mine are Yours, and Yours are Mine; and I have been glorified in them*" (John 17:10.) This is an interesting exchange in that Christ acknowledges that the disciples were from God and belonged to God in verse 9. But in verse 10, He calls them His own, then says, "But they're also Yours". I love how this seals our belonging. I'm not saying God and Jesus are fighting over us, but are simply emphasizing how much they both love us. "***And I have been glorified in them.***" This is an incredible statement by Christ. He speaks of the things which were not, but which should be as though they were. Christ anticipates His name will be glorified by the successful preaching still to come. I can't resist the similarity in Hebrews 11:1, "*Now faith is the assurance of things hoped for, the conviction of things not seen.*"

"*I am no longer in the world; and yet they themselves are in the world; and I come to You, Holy Father, keep them in Your name, the name which You have given Me, that they may be one even as We are*" (John 17:11). The disciples will need every ounce of Christ's intercession to be preserved in God's truth. Christ is praying for unity in their beliefs, for one body of believers, held together by the Holy Spirit so that their oneness would exactly resemble the oneness and unity that exists between Christ and the Father.

"*I have given them Your word; and the world has hated them, because they are not of the world, even as I am not of the world*" (John 17:14). It is fascinating that Christ speaks of the future as if it is the past. It is the same for you and me. When Christ went to the cross, He saw our future; He died for all our sin, past, present and future; He died for all our afflictions, present and future; and He died for all of our broken heartedness. (Please revisit chapter 1). All of those conditions are in the past to God; they have been dealt with two thousand years ago. Grace allows us to appropriate what has already been completed.

"*I do not ask You to take them out of the world, but to keep them from the evil one*" (John 17:15). The disciples still have an assignment to carry out. It will be fraught with danger and death, but God's plan requires that the Gospel be preached. Christ prays that Satan will not be allowed to destroy them as he did Judas. The Lord's Prayer He taught the disciples mirrors this sentiment, "Lead *us not into temptation, but deliver us from evil...*"

"*Sanctify them in the truth; Your word is truth*" (John 17:17). It is through the truth of God's word that leads others to salvation. How necessary it will become that the disciples are set apart for God's use in spreading the gospel.

"*As You sent Me into the world, I also have sent them into the world. For their sakes I sanctify Myself, that they themselves also may be sanctified in truth*" (John 17:18–19). Christ can intercede for the disciples because He is not asking them to do anything different than what He did. In verse 19, He is setting Himself aside for death in order that the disciples, in preaching the gospel of salvation, will be protected by the entire Messianic truth of Christ's crucifixion and resurrection.

"*I do not ask on behalf of these alone, but for those also who believe in Me through their word*" (John 17:20). This intercession will permeate throughout all the ages and bring salvation to every soul who believes in Jesus Christ. Even now, two thousand years later, we are still benefiting from Christ's unselfish sacrifice.

"*That they may all be one; even as You, Father, are in Me and I in You, that they also may be in Us, so that the world may believe that You sent Me*" (John 17:21). This prayer, this intercession was answered as early as in Acts 4:32, "*And the congregation of those who believed were of* ***one*** *heart and soul; and not one of them claimed that anything belonging to him was his own, but all things were common property to them.*" Christ is clear in the last part of verse 21; if the world believes in Jesus, say, only as a prophet, but not the Son of God, then it will be of no saving value to them.

"*The glory which You have given Me I have given to them, that they may be one, just as We are one. I in them and You in Me, that they may be perfected in unity, so that the world may know that You sent Me, and loved them, even as You have loved Me*" (John 17:22–23). The important thing to realize in these verses is that after verse 20, Christ is talking about all believers. We have received His glory, we are to be perfected in unity. This perfection allows us to live in Christ's peace, love, and grace.

The greatest identity shift in the history of the world is of course Jesus Christ leaving the heavenly kingdom as God, leaving the source of all creation, all wisdom, all creativity, all knowledge, to become man. In only this way could He once and for all save His and His Father's creation.

Isaiah 53:12b reads, "*Because He poured out Himself to death, and was numbered with the transgressors; yet He Himself bore the sin of many, and interceded for the transgressors.*" Isaiah says that Christ was numbered with the transgressors. It was a role He relished; He lived for them; He died for them. **His entire life, His ministry, His humiliation, His agony, His death, His Passion—all of it was intercession** for the transgressors; for you and me!

His Identity Shift took Him among the downtrodden, the sinful, the sick, and the lowly. He identified with them so that we now can identify with Him. We can identify with His risen holiness, His righteousness, His peace, His grace, and His Mercy. The Bible tells us He is now seated at the right hand of God—to do what? To continue making intercession for us.

Intercession Can Be Violent

Several years ago, my son was playing college baseball and was assigned to a summer league in Alaska between his freshman and sophomore year. His team had traveled to play in Kenai, a city on the Kenai Peninsula, which is the land mass on the south side of the Cook Inlet. One night, about midnight (our time), he called to tell me about the game and that he was currently fishing along the banks of the Kenai River. Of course, it was summertime and the salmon were running and there was plenty of daylight there. After a moment of silence, he suddenly let out a long "whoooooooooa." "What's going on?" I asked. "Dad! Just up the bank there's a big brown bear trying to catch some salmon!" My heart was in my mouth. "Get out of there!" I screamed inwardly to myself, not wanting to sound like an overprotective father.

All ended well, and it was a once-in-a-lifetime experience for him, but imagine what a momma bear would do if someone were closing in on her cubs. She would spare no fury to intercede. The intruder would *meet* up with a great deal of violence. The word *intercession* comes from the Hebrew word *to meet;* **Paga,** pronounced *paw-gah,* meaning "to impinge, by accident or by violence, or by importunity (persistence)." It also means "meet or intercession."[12]

Paga is used in several scriptures in the Old Testament and always refers to a rising up or slaying of someone. **Judges 8:21, 1**

Samuel 22:17, and **2 Samuel 1:15** all reveal stories of Gideon, King Saul and David, respectively, killing people.

The paga surrounding Christ's intercession and crucifixion is told graphically in the text of Matthew 27:

> *And Jesus cried out again with a loud voice, and yielded up His spirit. And behold, the veil of the temple was torn in two from top to bottom; and the earth shook and the rocks were split. The tombs were opened, and many bodies of the saints who had fallen asleep were raised; and coming out of the tombs after His resurrection they entered the holy city and appeared to many. Now the centurion, and those who were with him keeping guard over Jesus, when they saw the earthquake and the things that were happening, became very frightened and said, "Truly this was the Son of God!"* (Matt. 27:50–54)

Old Testament uses of the word "paga" pale in comparison to the intensity of the force that occurred at Calvary. When Christ interceded for mankind, **violence erupted; the earth shook; the sun previously hidden, appeared; the centurion was terrified; and Old Testament saints were resurrected**.

The impact of Christ's intercession is revealed in 1 John 3:8: "*The one who practices sin is of the devil; for the devil has sinned from the beginning. The Son of God appeared for this purpose, to* ***destroy*** *the works of the devil.*"

In fact, Satan took the beating of his life. **"Destroy"** in the Greek is the word, *Luo*. Strong's translates it like this. "To loosen, break, destroy, melt, dissolve or break down."[13] There are two meanings; one is legal, the other is physical.

The legal meaning of *luo* has to do with pronouncing or determining that something or someone is no longer bound. It also means to dissolve or void a contract or anything that legally binds. Jesus dissolved the legal hold Satan had over us and to make certain that we were no longer bound by his works. In fact, He voided the contract **breaking Satan's dominion over us**.

The physical meaning of *luo* is to dissolve or melt, break, beat something to pieces or untie something that is bound. There's an interesting scripture in 2 Peter 3:10, which uses the word ***luo***: "*But the day of the Lord will come like a thief, in which the heavens will pass away with a roar and the elements will be **destroyed** with intense heat, and the earth and its works will be burned up.*"

Jesus not only delivered us legally, but He also made certain that the literal consequences of those deliverances, violent as they were at the time, were manifested. He brought healing, set captives free, lifted oppression, and liberated those under demonic control.

Intercession is many things, but it is not placid or half-hearted. It is not something to be taken lightly or abandoned. We, through *prayers* and actions of intercession, *meet* **(*paga*)** the powers of darkness, enforcing the victory **(*luo*)** that Christ accomplished when He *met them in His work of intercession.*

Why do we continue to follow a defeated enemy?

When God pushed Satan out of heaven or "cast him out," Satan knew he could never defeat God or take His place, as had been his goal. (Please read Isaiah 14:12–15). From that moment on, Satan determined to get even with God by attacking God's people. For our part, we help him by being vulnerable to the sin of the flesh. We have a choice to follow good or to follow evil. One of my pastors made the comment that "there is so much sin in the world because we crave it." That's so true!

Satan is defeated, but not bound. First Peter 5:8 will warn you when Satan is attacking you, and James 4:7 will tell you how to send him packing.

10

Prayer Bowls

My wife Janelle and I brought home many memories of our trip to Alaska. We took a glacier cruise, watched sea otters playing in Prince William Sound, gawked at towering snow-covered mountains, experienced glaciers "calving" with an eerie cracking, fracturing sound, which gave you a couple of seconds to turn toward the noise and watch huge "boulders" of ice hurl themselves into the bay. We enjoyed daylight at midnight! In fact, my son's baseball team played in the Midnight Classic in Fairbanks. This is a baseball game played every year where kids face ninety plus mile-per-hour fastballs at the plate, and the game isn't allowed to start until midnight! The whole game is played without using the stadium lights! And yes, I would be remiss if I didn't mention the mouth-watering Haddock entrees. This meal with these fresh fish give "fish and chips" a whole new meaning! So many great memories!

God's Treasures

Are you like us, avid collectors? Do you keep memories of yesteryear? Do you have a special place in your home where you keep special things from your life? I would guess that the list of things that people collect are probably endless. My wife saves many of the things her students have given her over her years of teaching. My mom saved *every* card and *every* letter from her kids. If you are the parent of a child who plays sports, you likely have all of their team and individual pictures, trophies, uniforms, and equipment. If your child does well in school, you save all of their certificates, their awards for honor roll, principal's list, and so forth. If any of this applies to you, I would say yes, you are a collector.

Did you know that God is also a collector? Think about this; the One who calls all things that are visible and invisible as His own; the One who created the ocean tides and currents to stop exactly where He placed the shorelines; the One who measured the gravitational pull of one body of mass against another to be so precise that they would attract but not crash into each other; the One who put the spin to the earth's rotation so that we would have day and night; and the One who meticulously wove together the anatomy and physiology of our human bodies to work perfectly according to His plan… is a collector! What could *He* possibly collect? He owns it all! Yet, He who *owns everything, cherishes and collects* something that ***we bring into being***, something that ***we have created***, and something that is ***uniquely ours***. So think about this—He is collecting things about *His* children exactly the way we do with ours. Now I know where *we* get it from. We're not "pack rats" after all; we're just mimicking our Father's actions.

Pause with me and think about this for a minute. I've seen grown men and women drawing people who look like stick figures. Well, there's no problem with that; it's not a serious issue to be artistically challenged, but when you compare those creations with the real thing—the living, breathing specimens that God created—we see how great a chasm there is between God's creativity and ours. I see (and admire) people who plant seeds for flowers or trees in their gardens and faithfully water them every day; and then I see on a grander scale, the creation of fertile soil, millions of different seeds, the warmth of sunlight and the global weather movements that water God's gardens. I think back on the NASA programs, in particular the one where Neil Armstrong was the first man to walk on the moon, and appreciate how great a feat this was; but then I realize that Jesus was the first God to visibly walk on the earth. I'm not making the comparisons to put human efforts down; I admire all of man's creativity, but I am speechless when it comes to describing the majesty of Jehovah. So it gives me an incredible sense of awe to think that God would love, cherish, and keep something that *we* create.

Why? Why does God collect things? Why do *we* collect things? Isn't it because we treasure the memories, the times when these things happened in our life? Isn't it because these are the things that make us feel wonderful, needed, respected, and cared for? God created us to revere and enjoy the memories of those close to us, and the way they have impacted our lives. ***In similar fashion, God cherishes and collects the things from those who are close to Him***; the things *we* do that bring Him love, respect, honor or glory. You've likely guessed by now that it is ***our prayers*** that God collects and holds so dear to His heart.

Weather experts will tell you that no two snowflakes are alike. The prayers of God's children all around the world are so unique that no two of *them* are the same. Yet, as voluminous and different as they are, God keeps every one of them, keeps them—until He acts on them! How do I know this? Read on!

If you recall back in chapter 1, we discussed why it is important for us to know how much God loves us. We looked at the Hebrew word for "image" (*tselem*) and learned just how precisely God created us to resemble Himself. Without a solid base to understand who we are in God's eyes or how we fit in the grand scheme of things or how we are part of God's plans for creation and, to be more precise, how He cherishes us in His heart, we can never be confident that we have the status to coexist with God, to enjoy a full partnership with Him, much less believe that our prayers are heard and acted on.

An additional look at who we are.

Here's something to augment the "**tselem**" issue and give your mind something to really "chew" on: Yes, we are created in God's image, but it reaches even deeper than that. Look at Genesis 1:26: "Then God said, *'Let **Us** make man in **Our** image, according to **Our** likeness';*"—"**Us, Our, and Our**".

Who is God talking to? Angels? Nope, doubtful! Here's a clue. No, make that *three* clues. Look at Genesis 1: "*In the beginning, **God** created the heavens and the earth. The earth was formless and void, and darkness was over the surface of the deep, and the **Spirit of God** was moving over the surface of the waters*" (Gen. 1:1–2). Oh, okay. There was God and the Holy Spirit. That's the "Us", right? Almost. Let's read John 1: "*In the beginning was the Word, and the Word was with God, and the Word was God. He was in the beginning with God. All things came into being through Him, and apart from Him nothing came into being that has come into being*" (John 1:1–3).

There it is! **The Trinity!** Not convinced that John 1:1–3, the "Word" represents Christ? We're in agreement with the other Two though, aren't we? God and the Holy Spirit? One more Scripture then. "*For by Him (Christ) all things were created, both in the heavens and on earth, visible and invisible, whether thrones or dominions or rulers or authorities - all things have been created through Him and for Him. He is before all things, and in Him all things hold together*" (Col. 1:16–17).

This is important. If I had you convinced in chapter 1 about being made in the image of God and therefore able to have a say in things or a partnership with God, then what you are about to read will put you over the top. This will change your life! We are made in the image of God the Father, God the Son, and God the Holy Spirit! Parts of the Trinity make up our existence! But which is which?

The Holy Spirit

The first one is pretty straight forward. Our *spirit* is fashioned in the manner of the Holy Spirit. Our spirit has all of the qualities that we admire in the Holy Spirit. Until you accept Jesus Christ as your Savior, your spirit is dead to sin; but after accepting Christ, it comes alive in the Holy Spirit. We were created to enjoy and employ ***Love, Joy, Peace, Patience, Kindness, Goodness, Faithfulness, Gentleness, and Self-Control.*** It is important to realize that these qualities or "fruit" as Paul calls them are distributed by the Holy Spirit from His presence within us. They are not manifested as a result of something or some action that we do. They are fruit, not works. *Strong's* defines fruit as *karpos* a noun in the Greek. Paul uses "fruit" as appearing to be singular while we often think of this as "fruits" of the Spirit since there are nine of them. "Karpos" suggests that we are in possession of all nine qualities, controlled by the Holy Spirit.

God the Father

I believe that our *mind or soul* is most representative of God, the Father. Our minds have free will, an option to choose. It is the creative part of us, just like God. We all seem to have the ability to formulate something in our mind, to rationalize or reason over problems (Isa. 1:18) and many of us have the talent to manifest our mental creations; not on the scale of God, of course, but on a smaller scale that is similar to God's attributes. We have the ability to love, and hate (Ps. 5:5 and 11:5), just like God. Because we are made in God's image, we are able to have or reflect compassion, mercy, grace, fellowship, friendship, etc. There are a lot of qualities that God did not share with His creation. Things like Omniscience and Omnipotence. Our human nature shares *some* of God's attributes, but not all in its internal and external characteristics. Clearly, we are not an exact duplicate (of God).

God's Son, Jesus Christ

Upon creation, since Christ was to be the only "humanoid-looking" part of the Trinity; did *they* decide to make us in Christ's earthly physical image as we would know Him, so that our acceptance of Him would be facilitated because we could identify with His appearance? We are able to do many of the things that Christ did (John 14:12). We can visit the sick and the imprisoned. We lay hands on people, we evangelize and spread the gospel. We spend time speaking with Our Father in prayer. We are instructed to become "more Christlike!" "*For we are His workmanship, created in Christ Jesus for good works, which God prepared beforehand, that we should walk in them*" (Eph. 2:10).

This is how much God loved you when he created you; this is how much God continues to love you as you struggle with all that life throws at you. This partnership He desperately wants to have with you, including plans or "assignments" as I have called them in the past involve prayer. Because you now know just how close or similar to God you have been made, it should be easier for you to bring everything to Him. There's nothing about you that God doesn't know about, and there's nothing about the Trinity that you don't have some portion of. It's time, as we bring this book to a close, to draw a parallel between God's love for us and His love for our prayers.

Prayer Bowls

I want to look at two passages in Revelation, which will illustrate where God collects our prayers. Revelation 5 says:

> *And I saw between the throne (with the four living creatures) and the elders, a Lamb standing, as if slain, having seven horns and seven eyes, which are the seven Spirits of God* (Isa. 11:2) *sent out into all the earth. And He came and took the book out of the right hand of Him who sat on the throne. When He had taken the book, the four living creatures and the twenty four elders fell down before the Lamb, each one holding a harp* ***and golden bowls full of incense, which are the prayers of the saints.*** (Rev. 5:6–8; emphasis mine)

Revelation 8 continues,

> *Another angel came and stood at the altar, holding a golden censer; and much incense was given to him,* ***so that he might add it to the prayers of all the saints on the golden altar which was before the throne. And the smoke of the incense with the prayers of the saints, went up before God out of the angel's hand.*** (Rev. 8:3–4; emphasis mine)

Jentezen Franklin (an American Pastor, best-selling author, TV personality and musician) said about this Scripture, "*What a marvelous image! When you pray, you are filling the prayer bowls of heaven. In God's perfect timing, your prayers are mixed with the fire of God (His power) and cast back down to earth to change your situation... Even if you don't feel like anything is happening in the natural world, when you pray, you are filling the prayer bowls in the spirit realm. When they are full, they will tilt and pour out answers to your prayers!*"[14] (*The Amazing Discernment of Women* by Jentezen Franklin).

Most of us don't have a problem with lingering in prayer. Or, put another way—we don't pray for very long! A recent study shows that the average American spends eight minutes a day in prayer! At the other end of this spectrum, if you think that the more you pray, the more you will influence God to do something, then you have converted this very Holy Act of Prayer into an activity of works. Christians need to stay under Grace, not meander back into Law because of a lack of understanding.

James 5:16 says, "*The effectual fervent prayer of a righteous man availeth much.*" Pray with a diligent and righteous heart and believe that the prayer bowls are filling up and that God will tip one of them over and pour fire down on to the earth!

All of us who have prayed know what the act of praying looks like on earth. Some will put their hands together in front of their face, fingers pointing toward heaven; others will put their arms up as if signaling a touchdown; still others will get down on their knees, and so forth. But the one feature of praying that seems to be common with all of the above is closing one's eyes and bowing one's head. We can see the act, but we can't see the prayer. We don't know where the prayer goes. Does it even leave the body? How does it escape? We hope it does. We hope it goes up—up toward heaven, up toward God, but there's no way to tell, visually—until now. Now we *know* where all those unseen prayers end up. They're right there, in golden bowls, next to God—exactly where we wanted them to be.

The world will tell us there is no ear to hear when we speak our words of request and desire—that our petitions merely float off into the air, and that is the end of them. But these two passages from the book of Revelation show that the prayers of believers are not lost. Instead, we get a glimpse from the other side and find our prayers caught and preserved in *golden bowls!* You may have all of your memories on a dusty shelf, stuck in a drawer or photo album somewhere; but God keeps His treasures in bowls of gold until He acts on them! That thought is very comforting and beautiful.

Christ exhorts us to not use meaningless repetition when we pray. *On the surface this may seem contradictory to the concept of Prayer Bowls. Christ is addressing substance over matter. Here are some other Scriptures that extol repetition in prayer:*

"*And they cried one to another, and said; Holy, Holy, Holy, the Lord GOD of hosts, all the earth is full of His glory*" (Isa. 6:3). *These are the Seraphim* ***repetitively*** *praising God.*

"*And leaving them he went back again, and prayed a third time, saying the same words over*" (Matt. 26:36–44). *Jesus Christ Himself in repetitious prayer. Can we do less?*

"Now *it came to pass in those days, that He went out to the mountain to pray,* ***and continued all night in prayer to God***" (Luke 6:12; emphasis mine).

11

Prayers, Incense, and God's Power

Incense

Perhaps just as important as Prayer Bowls is the other feature of those Scriptures in Revelation—the **incense**. Some time ago, an e-mail was circulating asking the recipient to list his or her favorite smell before sending it on to all in their address book. There were some interesting notations: the smell of rain, freshly cut grass, pipe tobacco, coffee, a pine forest, the salty smell of the ocean, a cozy fire, flowers, new puppies, babies' skin, leather, and so on. I'm sure you can add several of your own.

It seems that God's favorite smell is the burning of incense. Walk with me a minute and let's unpack this. I want to relate the following Scriptures and discourse on incense to the activities of the provisional temple that God ordered built in the desert during the exodus of the Jews from Egypt. You will see some incredible foreshadowing regarding Christ, and I want you to notice how deep and intentional God made this.

Incense is a ***symbol*** for the prayers of God's people. King David says in Psalm 141:2, "*May my prayer be counted as incense before You; the lifting up of my hands as the evening offering.*" In the temple, the people would gather to pray in the place for worship while the priest burned incense on the golden altar. Luke 1:10 speaks of John the Baptist's father, Zacharias entering the Holy Place of the temple to burn incense, "*And the whole multitude of the people were in prayer outside at the hour of the incense offering.*"

Prayer and incense seem to be inextricably linked—at least in the Old Testament. The burning incense would rise upward in a cloud of smoke and biblically, clouds were often used as a sign of God's presence. Exodus 13:22 tells us that the Israelites were *led* by a pillar of cloud; Exodus 40:34 says that a cloud *covered* the Tabernacle, and the glory of the Lord *filled* it; During the Transfiguration of *Christ*, a cloud appears and the Voice of God is heard from *within* it (Matt. 17:5). And finally, Acts 1:9 tells us that Jesus is *taken up into* a cloud. We see then that just as prayer and incense are linked, so are incense and clouds and to go one step further, so are clouds and God, or at least the Spirit of God! Kind of tuck this in the back of your mind as I lead us through the importance of incense in the next few pages.

In ancient times, *incense* was used to sweeten and purify the air before an important visitor arrived (only an *important* visitor, because incense was very expensive and could only be used on special occasions). Christ taught us that He is in the midst of us wherever two or three are gathered in His Name (Matt. 18:20). Who is a more important visitor than our Savior? Our Lord may not be physically visible, but He has promised to be present. The beautiful aroma of incense (marrying ancient times to present day) is associated with Christ in the following Scriptures. Ephesians 5:2 suggests that incense around God's throne reminds *Him* of the presence of Christ as our prayers are presented: "*And walk in love, just as Christ also loved you and gave Himself up for us, an offering and a sacrifice to God as a **fragrant aroma**.*"

A prophecy in the book of Malachi tells us that God is done with the offerings of bulls and goats on the altars. They have been replaced by grain that is pure (the unspotted lamb of Jesus Christ); and the smoke from those animal sacrificial offerings will be replaced by incense. "*For from the rising of the sun even to its setting, My name will be great among the nations, and in every place incense is going to be offered to My name, and a grain offering that is pure; for My name will be great among the nations, says the Lord of hosts*" (Mal. 1:11).

The *apostle* Paul, possibly referring to the fact that Christ's body after His crucifixion, was wrapped with linens and *incense*, calls us the *aroma* of Christ to God.

> *But thanks be to God, who always leads us in triumph in Christ, and* ***manifests through us the sweet aroma of Him*** *in every place, For* ***we are a fragrance of Christ to God*** *among those who are being saved and among those who are perishing; to the one an aroma from death to death, to the other* ***an aroma from life to life.*** *And who is adequate for these things?* (2 Cor. 2:14–16; emphasis mine)

All of these passages reveal how incense links the past with the present; links God to the prayers of His people through the presence of His Son, Jesus Christ.

I'd like us to follow the parallels between the Old Testament and the New Testament (the foreshadowing of Christ in the older Scriptures that I mentioned earlier) because there is a seamless continuum of God's yearning to be close to His people, ending of course with Christ's sacrifice, which secures our eternal dwelling place and closeness with God.

We can see some of the very first attempts that God used in order to draw close to the Israelites during the exodus. These were a people who easily fell away from any trust or any acknowledgment of God, despite what they had witnessed since leaving Egypt. We have a propensity to act in a similar manner, especially when times are tough. For this reason, I want you to see, not only how much God cares about you, but how He safeguards your communications with Him as well. Watch how He did this during the exodus, and if the thought crosses your mind that, "that was then, now is now", just remember, He is the same yesterday, today and forever (Heb. 13:8).

As I have said earlier, I have doubts that the Hebrew nation coming out of Egypt, now wandering in the desert, believed in or knew their God. When God was "recruiting" Moses to go and bring the Hebrews out of Egypt, Moses protested five different times and on this occasion, he wonders if they will recognize who God is.

> *Then Moses said to God, "Behold I am going to the sons of Israel, and I shall say to them, 'The God of your fathers has sent me to you.' Now they may say to me, '**What is His name?**' What shall I say to them?" God said to Moses, **"I AM WHO I AM"**; and He said, "Thus you shall say to the sons of Israel, 'I AM has sent me to you.'"* (Exod. 3:13–14; emphasis mine) (Please note that "I AM WHO I AM" is the inner meaning of Yahweh—"*I am the One who is*".)

After God led the Hebrew nation out of Egypt, we find this mass of humanity (one to two million people plus livestock!) at the foot of Mount Sinai. As we will read in a few pages, God has tried over and over to be their God and to show them great and wondrous signs, but they are a "stiff-necked people", to use God's expression for them. So He instructs Moses to build a portable temple, explaining "why" in Exodus 25:8, "*Let them construct a sanctuary for Me that **I may dwell among them**.*"

The Sanctuary

The temple or sanctuary consisted of four main areas. The peripheral boundaries were an open area where the people would come to worship. The inner court was the location where the priests sacrificed the animal offerings on the altar of atonement. Inside the temple were two areas: *The Holy Place*. The larger of the two rooms in the Tabernacle, which could be entered often and, in fact, was entered daily by the Levitical priests in order to carry out the various duties of worship as mediators for the people of Israel. The second area was *the holy of holies*, often called the Holiest. This was the place where God's Shekinah Glory was actually present, and it was entered only once a year by the High Priest on the Day of Atonement. This act only occurred after he had been made ritually clean so that he might not die in God's presence.

The typology of the High Priest entering the Holy of Holies is rich in meaning: **(1)** ***Only he was the mediator between God and His people.*** But before the priest could begin serving his people, he had to be sin free. **(2)** ***A sinful person could not enter into this room***, because his sin would lead to death right there in the very presence of God. This priest had a rope tied to his ankle so that he could be pulled out in case he died by God's hand. This tells us a lot about how much God hates sin. The High Priest could enter in and be acceptable to God, only if he obeyed God's laws regarding all the rituals of cleansing. **(3)** ***Only then could he offer atonement for the sins of his people***.

Under the new covenant you and I have with God, through His son Jesus Christ, we can see that God has not changed regarding His position on sin and sinful man. Our righteousness is gifted to us through the righteousness of Jesus; our High Priest! Relating to the points above, **(1a)** ***Instead of the Israelite's High Priest being the only mediator between them and God, now Jesus Christ is our eternal mediator with God; (2a) Instead of a common man, as a High Priest ritually cleansed free from sin, entering into the Holy of Holies, our High Priest Jesus Christ, always without sin, enters into the very presence of God on our behalf.*** And finally, because the blood of bulls and goats only dealt with sin temporarily and did not remove sin for all time, the High Priest could only offer atonement for one year. **(3a)** ***Our High Priest, by offering up the blood of the unblemished lamb—His own body as a sacrifice—atoned***

our sins for all time, past, present, and future. This is explained in Hebrews 9:1–15.

Today, the temple and the Shekinah Glory dwell inside of us. Listen to Paul's explanation in 1 Corinthians 3:16, "*Do you not know that you are **a temple** of God and that the **Spirit of God dwells in you?***" Just as this early Hebrew nation did not know or understand that God wanted this temple built so that He could "***dwell among them***", many Christians today are not aware, do not understand, or do not believe that we are also filled with the "***shekinah***" glory of God. That's right! We are filled with the very light and glory of God! Not convinced? The Greek word that Paul used for the word "temple" in 1 Corinthians 3:16 is "***Naos***". *Strong's* defines it as *"the sanctuary in the temple, into which only the priests could lawfully enter... the proper habitation of God"*[15] **Naos** refers to the *holy of holies.* The Shekinah glory of God now dwells in the holy of holies within us! This is the "living water" that we spoke of earlier in the book!

Another foreshadowing involves the veil in the old temple. The sacred area in this temple was separated from the *Holy Place* by a **veil whose purpose was to restrict access to God**. But when Jesus Christ became our High Priest, the veil that stands between the two rooms was torn from top to bottom (Matt. 27:51) and both rooms became one because of the ripped veil. Hebrews 10:19–20 tells us that this ripped veil that provided us with access to the very presence of God was represented by the gashes and tearing that the spears made in Christ's body as He hung on the cross. "*Therefore, brethren, since we have confidence to enter the holy place by the blood of Jesus, by a new and living way which He inaugurated for us through the veil, that is, His flesh.*" Hebrews 10:21–22 continues by saying that now the believer, ushered in by his High Priest, Jesus Christ, may be united with the Father by the Son: "*And since we have a great priest over the house of God, let us draw near with a sincere heart in full assurance of faith, having our hearts sprinkled clean from all evil conscience and our bodies washed with pure water.*"

For me, this illustrates clearly the scriptural claim in Hebrews 13:8, "*Jesus Christ is the same yesterday and today and forever.*" God created the Temple—a place for His people to assemble and worship;

today, the church (His people) worship together; God established a holy intercessor, the priest, to represent His people and offer atonement for their sins; today, we have *the one and only* intercessor, Jesus Christ, who became the perfect sacrifice in offering His people forgiveness of sins; God created a Holy Place where His Shekinah Glory dwelled; today, that glory, that holy place dwells within us.

The French have an expression: "*le plus que change, le moins de change*". (Hope I remembered my high school French correctly) It means "*the more things change, the less things change*". There are radical differences between Old Testament worship and regulations and New Testament, New Covenant worship; but really, all of the theology and regulation aside, God prepared a way for His people to come close to Him then, and He has made a way for His people to come close to Him now.

Let's continue exploring the significance of the incense. Inside the Holy Place, next to the veil that separated God from His people, was the ***golden incense-altar***. This was the altar of prayer.

> *Moreover, you shall make an altar as a place for burning incense… You shall put this altar in front of the veil that is near the ark of the testimony, in front of the mercy seat that is over the ark of the testimony, where I will meet with you. Aaron shall burn fragrant incense on it; he shall burn it every morning when he trims the lamps. When Aaron trims the lamps at twilight, he shall burn incense. There shall be perpetual incense before the Lord throughout your generation.* (Exod. 30:1, 6–8)

These passages make me curious as to why God wanted Aaron burning incense morning and night, or as God says, "*Perpetual incense.*"

Here's a thought. I wonder if it was just one of many events that God created to convince this stubborn people that He *was* their God. Instead of parting the Red Sea, He could have put all of them into a deep sleep and instructed His angels to carry them across to the other side; He could have enlightened Moses with directions for leading the people through the desert, but instead His Glory appeared in a pillar of cloud—even lighting up at night—to prove to His people that He was with them; He could have created great basins of fresh water for the people but instead He had Moses strike his rod against a stone (twice) to produce water; He made the top of Mount Sinai billow with smoke and glow with fire to prove that He was up there with their leaders.

It seems like God is bending over backwards to convince this stubborn bunch of people that He is their God and He wants to care for them, even "***dwell among them.***" So, what about the incense? A couple of pages back, I mentioned that, although we can see people praying, we can't see any evidence of a prayer. Is it possible that God needed the people to *see* evidence of their prayers ascending upwards so they would believe that they were communicating with their God? And, after everything He's been through with them, wouldn't this incense add sweet aromas to their prayers allowing Him to enjoy His children's efforts to acknowledge Him, to accept Him? This foreshadowing is revealed in our Revelation scripture. The redeemed are represented as "*holding a harp and golden bowls full of incense, which are the prayers of the saints*" (Rev. 5:8). Your prayers and my prayers, all of earth's supplications rise up into heaven as sweet incense, as a holy fragrance before God. Just like the prayers of the Hebrew nation, God is showing us, thousands of years later, that our prayers are in the very same way, rising up to Him along with the incense.

In many ways, we are just like the Israelites; grumbling about things, self-centered, not sure if God is listening to us, but these Scriptures show us clearly that God receives every one of our groans, every whimper, every cry, every petition, every request, and every intercession. He keeps them safe in His most precious and sacred containers, the golden bowls, so that none of them will be lost!

Something to think about before the incense kicks in.

Even though our prayers are like a fragrance to God, we need to be aware that there is an ingredient to prayer that rests fully with us. By making sure that we are committed to offer these precious "*collec-*

tions" in a manner as worthy as possible, we can begin to recognize the continuing intercession and abundant worthiness that Christ brings before the throne of God as He presents our requests. If our prayers were to stand alone—that is, without Christ's intercession—we would see that they are replete with unholy baggage. This lack of holiness manifests itself within three different periods of time as we engage in the activity of prayer.

1. **Pre-Prayer: Unfit for Worship**.

First, many of us come to the Father, *even before our prayer begins,* unfit for worship with an unprepared heart. Our attitudes may be bogged down with "life". We are angry, confused, or impatient with the world, with our circumstances. There seems to be no answers, no escape, and no prospects for change. Perhaps the best way I can illustrate would be like this: A discussion with your spouse begins to heat up; old hurts are revisited and before you know it, the two of you are in a yelling match. Just about that time, the kids run in and say, "Daddy!" or "Mommy!" Without breaking stride with your emotions, your tone of voice continues and you turn to them and yell, "***What?***"

They didn't deserve that. You were unfit for dialogue with them. You hadn't prepared your heart to deal with a different circumstance. And the same thing happens between us and God. The solution is very simple—just take a few minutes before you begin your prayer and let your mind contemplate who He is and how eager He is to hear from you.

Remember how the Israelites behaved after leaving Egypt when they were in the wilderness? It was continuous grumbling. Even if they had gone before God, their hearts would have been hard. They felt that He had brought them into the wilderness to die. They wanted only to return to bondage and slavery under Pharaoh. Their only prospect for escape or change was preferring to worship a golden calf instead of worshipping a God they didn't care for very much. In their minds, if they believed strongly enough, *their* idol would overpower the God of Moses and set them free. They too, were unfit for worship.

2a. Wandering thoughts during worship.

Many times when we are in the very midst of our devotion, meandering and unrelated thoughts creep in and interrupt our prayers. Suddenly, we'll start thinking about and planning our day, recalling all the things that we have to do, or we will remember there's a show we wanted to see on television that starts at nine, so we take a peek at our watch. And our worship flees. I've actually wandered so far from the sanctity of the moment that I have fallen asleep before finishing a prayer. With practice, we can strengthen our time with God and minimize this.

2b. Conflicted hearts during worship.

When God sees *neglect* or *conflict* in our hearts, He reacts accordingly.

- Proverbs 21:13 says, "*If a man shuts his ears to the cry of the poor, he too will cry out and not be answered.*"
- Sometimes as we go through life, we are so invested in our own agendas, we knowingly and stubbornly resist God's urgings. Zechariah 7:13 says, "*When I called, they did not listen; so when **they** called, I would not listen, says the Lord Almighty.*"

As you begin prayer and worship within "the new holy of holies", be mindful of how great our God is; be mindful that He gets things done on earth through His people and look around to see where you can help. Remember, no matter how old, how beaten up, how sick you may be, God still has an assignment for you.

3. **Doubt as we close our worship.**

At other times, just as our petition is closing, we let doubt overtake the faithfulness of God. Did we pray enough? Were we really clear about the issue? Does God really care enough to help me? These doubts withdraw the sacrifice we have just offered.

- "*But when he asks, he must believe and not doubt, because he who doubts is like a wave of the sea, blown and tossed by the wind. That man should not think he will receive anything from the Lord*" (James 1:6–7).

And sometimes, self-indulgence wades in James 4:3, "*When you ask, you do not receive, because you ask with wrong motives, that you may spend what you get on your pleasures.*"

The Reverend C.H. Spurgeon preached:

> *The sins of our holiest thoughts are, alone, enough to condemn us! Alas, how hard it is to begin, continue, and end a prayer in the Spirit! If any one of our prayers were put into the scales of the sanctuary, alone and of itself, the only verdict upon it must be it is weighed in the balances and found wanting. No, my Brothers and Sisters, the prayers of the saints, of themselves considered, would rather be an offense unto Divine holiness than a sweet savor unto God. Our consolation lies in this - that our beloved Intercessor who stands before God for us, even Christ Jesus - possesses such an abundance of precious merit that* ***He puts fragrance into our supplications and imparts a delicious aroma to our prayers!*** *He makes our intercessions to be, through His merit, what they could not have been without it - acceptable before the Majesty of Heaven.*[16]

J.R. Miller wrote in 1888 about the sweet fragrance of prayer:

> *There is an exquisite beauty in the thought that* ***true prayer is fragrance to God*** *as it rises from the golden altars of believing, loving hearts. The pleadings and supplications of his people on the earth - are wafted up to him from lowly homes, from humble sanctuaries, from stately cathedrals, from sick-rooms and from the darkened chambers of sorrow - as the breath of flowers is wafted to us from rich gardens and fragrant fields. Perfume is the breath of flowers, the sweetest expression of their inmost being and an exhalation of their very life. It*

> *is a sign of perfect purity, health and vigor; it is a symptom of a full and joyous existence - for disease and decay and death yield, not pleasant - but revolting odors - and, as such, fragrance is in nature, what prayer is in the human world. Prayer is the breath of life, the expression of the soul's best, holiest and heavenliest aspirations, the sign and token of its spiritual health. The natural counterparts of the prayers that rise from the closet and the sanctuary, are to be found in the fragrant breathings, sweetening all the air, from gardens of flowers, from clover-crofts or thymy hillsides or shady pine woods, and which seem to be grateful, unconscious acknowledgments from the heart of Nature - for the timely blessings of the great world-covenant, dew to refresh and sunshine to quicken.*[17]

It is fascinating to examine who we are in God's sight. Still prone to sin at any given moment, even though we in ourselves feel pure and whole and righteous, God knows that our physical nature is surrounded by and wrapped up in the squalor and filth of an immoral, selfish world. Our Father accepts us because He views us through the prism, through the filter, of Jesus Christ. Through Him, God sees us as the righteous, holy, finished work of His Son at Calvary. God's goodness meets all our needs; His mercy covers all our faults. Often, our prayers may seem to remain long unanswered, for some blessings are so rich that they cannot be prepared for us in a day, but we may be sure that they are not lost nor forgotten. They are sacredly treasured and are always before God, and in due time, they will receive gracious and wise answer.

"*Then the angel took the censer and filled it with the fire of the altar, and threw it to the earth; and there followed peals of thunder and sounds and flashes of lightning and an earthquake*" (Rev. 8:5).

And a prayer was answered.

And now for you faithful readers, two bonus chapters that will provide the peace and deliverance we all so badly need.

12

Entering His Rest

The Opposite of Rest

It was Monday, two days before Christmas 2013. I arrived home late that night, about 10:00 p.m. and went straight to the fridge to get some ice for my water bottle. It had been a very long and tiring day, and I was ready to skip the evening news and go directly to bed. Out of the corner of my eye, I noticed the small blinking light on our home phone. A message! Should I pick it up or wait until morning? Not many people call us at home—just telemarketers. I decided to pick it up and the message was chilling: "*This is Sarah at Dr. Wilson's office. We have just received the radiology report on Janelle's brain scan and you need to get to an Emergency Room right away!*"

I'm not sure how to describe the exact feeling when your heart seems to drop into your stomach and you get this wave of chills sweeping over you; and life seems to stand still. But if you've experienced it, you know what I mean, and that's exactly how I felt—momentarily paralyzed by devastating news.

Seventy-seven hours earlier.

It was the last weekend before Christmas, 5:00 p.m., Friday night. We had just ordered a pizza and were sitting waiting for it when my wife's cell phone rang. "*Hello? About ten minutes. Okay!*" She looked at me and said, "*That was radiology; they want me to come back right away.*"

That's about the worst news I had received in my life up until the next worst news coming our way fifteen minutes later, and the next worst news still to come fifteen hours later.

The rush hour traffic wasn't too bad, and we were soon before the technician who was handing us the films and the disks they had made of my wife's brain. She had two brain bleeds in her brain stem, and we were instructed to get to the Emergency Room right away.

Janelle had worked the whole week, wrapping things up before Christmas break and sending her third grade class home for the holidays. A painful hip that had been bothering her for weeks caused her to make a doctor's appointment at the beginning of the week. This crazy confluence of events picked up another rider when she mentioned to the doctor that the right side of her face had gone numb for a couple of days and was now just centered under her eye socket. He ordered an MRI of her brain. Because of school, she wasn't able to have that done until 4:00 p.m. on this Friday night. Just reflecting back on that week and what could have gone wrong scares me even now. I mean, she had packed boxes and moved desks that week in her classroom!

We took the report and the disks across the street to Paradise Valley Hospital Emergency Room where the ER doctor forwarded her images to a neurosurgeon for review. Since PVH did not have a neurology department, this neurosurgeon sent instructions that she go home and call him Monday morning to make an appointment. But, he cautioned, if there was any change of feeling before then, she was to get to a facility with neurosurgical capabilities.

It's during times like this that caring Christians will go to prayer for you; but what do *you* do? Where do all the emotions you're experiencing go while *you* enter into prayer? Where did they go for me?

Well, they stayed with me. My wife and I went home, tried to get some sleep knowing in our hearts that Monday and that phone call was an eternity away; knowing that we were just beginning a long, difficult and most likely, life-changing period in our marriage. And what if she were to have a stroke while we were waiting for Monday to come?

We struggled with rest that night; me in this fog of trying to sort it all out, oscillating between prayer, confusion, planning, anxiety, reciting scripture, etc., and her trying to determine if anything was feeling different in her head. We had *anything but rest*—physical or spiritual.

Sometime, very early Saturday morning, perhaps around five thirty, she told me there was a tingling feeling in the back of her head. So this was how our procrastination would end. No longer could we pretend there wouldn't be a change in this issue. No longer could we avoid further medical diagnosis. We had to face this thing head on, knowing full well it could lead to brain surgery.

In my life, I've had hernia surgeries, tonsils removed, cataract surgery, a heart attack, and the insertion of a stent in a heart artery. But brain surgery? How does one's mind even grasp the enormity, complexity, and danger of that?

My wife, Janelle, handled it the best. With determination and a matter-of-fact bravery, she said, "I've already paid one ER two hundred fifty dollars and come away with nothing. I'm not going to pay two hundred fifty dollars to another and leave without them fixing my problem." She knew the path she had to take; face this thing head on and don't leave without getting it solved. My mind raced to those verses in Ephesians about putting on the full armor of God (Eph. 6:11–17). When you read this passage, look for something that protects your back. You won't find anything. It's like God is saying, "If you turn your back on your problems as if they didn't exist, I can't protect you. You need to walk with Me and we'll face your issues head-on."

The ER at Barrow's Neurological Institute took the brain scans they needed that Saturday and admitted her into ICU that afternoon scheduling her for surgery Monday morning. That was a long wait for us. Saturday to Monday just hanging around with nothing to do but try not to give in to fear.

The Challenge That Tests Your Faith

Faith struts along just fine, thank you, when you are in charge of what it looks like; how you display it and how you pursue it. You show up for church on a regular basis, belong to a Bible study, tithe every week, and if asked about your beliefs, you would enthusiastically reply that you are a Christian.

But how do you respond when your faith is taken out of your hands, out of your everyday routine? How does your practice of "casual faith", if I may use that phrase just for comparison, hold up when it is appropriated or hijacked and placed into the hands of "life-changing circumstances"? How do you respond when your faith is challenged to go deeper?

The next day and a half for me was a time to find out where my faith was at. I didn't realize it at the time, but it was also a time when God decided to teach me a few things about Grace. You see, this book was already finished and published as an e-book. Apparently, God wasn't happy with it and instructed me to add two more chapters. You are going to be the recipient of my anxiety and my new, God-given knowledge. So buckle up!

I hadn't planned to spend the four days before Christmas testing my faith. But then, none of us plan how our faith will react to disaster. The expression "*You can't climb a smooth mountain*" rolled around in my head. It has to do with faith. In other words, if the mountains in your life were smooth, you couldn't climb them because there are no footholds, no crevices to put your hands into to secure your position, nothing to rely on. Nothing for your faith to cling to.

In similar fashion, faith can't be tested away from the battlefield. It can't be fortified without testing. I had no idea what was looming in my future; in *our* future. There didn't seem to be any footholds. When they did show up, however, the mountain became less smooth, less intimidating. The footholds came from some unexpected places and left an immoveable, unshakeable peace that I want you to have when your mountains get "smooth," when you need to find a foothold, when "casual faith" doesn't cut it.

Strengthening Your Faith

I want you to know that I learned this lesson during my crisis which meant I had to go through the anguish of it all until the lesson took hold within me. My goal is to give you the answer, even though life is good for you right now, so that you can be prepared when life throws that nasty curve ball at you. You don't need to yield to events that bring "unrest" and to challenges that test your "every day" faith.

Let's look at Paul's advice about faith:

Romans 10:17 says this about faith: "*So faith comes from hearing, and hearing by the word of Christ.*"

Faith doesn't come by "***having heard***". *P*erhaps you are a believer; perhaps you ***have*** heard the Gospel, ***have*** heard about the need for faith; ***have*** heard about the resurrection and eternal life. The word ***hearing*** in Romans 10:17 is in the *present tense,* not the past tense. If you want to build and strengthen your faith—even if it is to simply apply it to a specific event—you have to be in the words of Jesus, in the Bible, in the sermon, in the televangelist's presentation—***often!*** Faith, like a muscle, has to be exercised as often as possible because we just don't know when our world will collapse.

And so, even though this telephone message Monday night chilled me, it came ***twelve hours after*** Janelle had been wheeled into surgery, nine hours ***after*** she had gone to recovery, and seven hours ***after*** I had a chance to talk with her once again back in her ICU room. It came ***after*** we were informed that the surgery had gone beautifully; ***after*** her brain stem had returned to its normal position, causing the numbness to disappear and ***after*** the danger had passed.

It was as if I was standing simultaneously at both ends of this time continuum. At the beginning of it, I was terrified or as I said, "Chilled" at the news; and at the end of it, elated to be looking back over it, saying, "This phone message frightens me, but we've climbed the mountain; we've seen the neurosurgeon; he's done the surgery; and she is recovering beautifully. It's behind us."

How Damaging and Unproductive Is Worry and Anxiety?

Harvey Mackay wrote an article in the *Arizona Republic* about worrying and said this: *"I recently received a cartoon from a friend that showed a psychiatrist having a session with her patient. She says, 'you worry too much… it doesn't do any good.'" And the patient answers, "It does for me… ninety-five percent of the things I worry about never happen!"*

Mackay's article goes on to say that "worry is the most unproductive of all human activities." He uses a neat metaphor to illustrate the futility: "You can't saw sawdust!" In case that didn't have the desired impact on you, here's a couple more. You can't squeeze lemonade; and you can't stir paint that's already on the wall!

Worrying is a strong indication of ***our self-righteousness***, and we are all guilty. When we worry and take the burden of our situations on to our own shoulders, we actually deny that God is *in control.* We deny that He is able or willing to *take control.* We even deny that God loves us enough to get us through our situation. We put our "*sovereignty*", our *self-righteousness* above His. We put our "*works*" above His grace! That's a dangerous place to be, folks. How can God work when we tell Him, "*It's okay. I got this?*" *Or* "*It's okay, I'd rather worry?*" How can we find the help we need when we, in effect are saying, "*My worrying and fretting are greater and mean more to me than your ability or desire to help me.*" And even worse, we are in fact saying, "*My circumstances are greater than my faith! And my reaction to them is so much stronger than your Mercy!*"

I wonder if we worry so that we can get used to all the dread by experiencing it before it happens; or perhaps we worry because we can't get our minds around the fact that there are unknowns in our existence, and we don't like that! Worrying is like a swimmer in trouble in the ocean. He is fighting so hard to avoid going under that the lifeguard can't get a good grip on him; can't begin to pull him to safety. Oftentimes, this struggle is so violent; the lifeguard is taken under and can't escape the imperiled man's grip. However, when the swimmer relaxes and lets the lifeguard help him, his safety is assured.

This is what happens to us when we relax and let God provide our rest. The whole reason for His rest is to allow us to appropriate His grace; to relax in His Provision, to hear the promptings He is giving us. If we ignore it, we will succumb to our ***unrest***, our fears, our illnesses, and our poverties.

How beautiful it is to be at the beginning of your odyssey, facing it with the calm and peace as if you were "looking back" on it as I was with this phone message. Philip Yancey, Christian author who has sold more than fourteen million books worldwide, said, "*I have learned that faith means trusting in advance what will only make sense in reverse.*"

The whole reason for God's rest is to allow us to be at peace while He takes care of His part. Without faith, neither will happen. "Well that's easy for you to say, Pastor, you're taking a phone message after the fact and claiming that it is restful to be looking back on the situation."

"That's correct, but I had to learn, and God had to teach me how to get there. And now I am going to teach you."

Faith and the Word Bring You into God's Rest

Christians should always be within God's rest. But we're not. We are always tuned into the world. In any twenty-four-hour period, we get far more input from the world than we get from our faith or our study of the word (unless we make a concentrated effort to be in the word). Cable News morning noon and night; Facebook and Twitter; even the drive to work can produce way too much drama. We react to shocking news stories, Wall Street ups and downs, sports scores, and of course, family and health concerns. The process of entering God's Rest begins when we realize that we are overwhelmed and inundated by the world. We are allowing ourselves to be defeated by things that have already themselves been defeated. When we begin this journey into God's rest, we go through some stages:

1. **Self-righteousness**. This is where we are when we decide to make a change. Our autonomy or "free choice" has conditioned us to become self-reliant. We train ourselves to only call on God for the "big" things in life. We see situations from *our point of view,* or from *the world's point of view.* We take a position that reflects our own **self-righteousness**. It's either a position of fear and worry or a position of "I can handle this". It's the same self-righteousness that caused God to give the law in the first place. In this condition, we will never find a state of rest or peace, only "what ifs" and "that's beyond my control". This scene usually results in cries of, "***God, where are you?***" Sound familiar?
2. **Grace**. Under grace, we begin to realize and accept that "He who is with us is greater than those things that are not." The events of the world and the chaos surrounding you are not "***with you***". They are decidedly "***against you!***" And, believe it or not, ***those events and that chaos could care less about you!*** The only thing that is bigger than you and bigger than all your problems is Grace. What makes Grace so nice is that ***Grace cares.*** It allows us to give all of the issues to God. Entering His rest means there are no "monsters" under the bed, no giants to slay. The fight is not in our hands, it is with the One who has *every part of our lives in His hands, not just this one issue.*
3. **In the Presence Of**. If you are able to enter the rest that God has provided for all who believe, you will find that *the elation of the peace of His presence washes away the fear of the unknown.* Remember, it's only unknown to you. When Adam and Eve walked with God, they were oblivious to sin and worldly events; after they sinned, they realized their nakedness and hid from God; the weight of the world on their shoulders. When Judas walked with Jesus, he walked in peace; after betraying His Lord, he hung himself out

of shame and regret. When Peter walked on water, he was concentrating on his Master; when he turned to the fears and threats of the world by noticing the danger around him, he began to sink.

How Do We Enter His Rest?

If you go back in chapter 6, or better still, review John 20:19, you will see that even in the darkest moments of your situation, Christ is already in your midst; already bringing you His peace. Unless you are able to manifest His presence into *your* senses, into *your* reality, into *your* "here and now", you won't feel the peace He comes with and your anxiety will prevail.

The day before Janelle's surgery, I reached out to an old college chum. We have been close friends for over fifty years. His father was a highly respected surgeon at Mary Hitchcock Hospital in Hanover, New Hampshire, and my friend had intimate knowledge of hospital and medical protocols, procedures, and what you might call panic-free reactions under stress.

He came with his peace during that phone call when he said, "*Clarkie, to you this is the most frightening thing in the world, but to the doctors and nurses, it's everyday life; it's neither complex nor frightening to them.*"

I clung to that statement; it was my gateway to the rest and peace I needed so desperately. This was the first part of that "smooth" mountain becoming a little jagged that I talked about. It came from an unexpected source.

And therein lies the beginning of entering into His rest—the first baby steps to unlocking the peace we need under duress:

Give it to, and rely on, the power and presence of the individuals who can control the situation.

It may begin with the medical team, or the financial team, or the conflict resolution team, but ultimately, it transcends to the One who controls the members of those teams. So pray for those people to be firmly in God's hands.

Realize that the John 20:19 miracle is already happening in your life, and the manifestation of Christ and His peace is closer than you think. If you think back to chapter 2 or just go back and reread it, you will see that Jesus ***knew*** that Lazarus had died before any word came out of Bethany. I suggested that if Christ knew that Lazarus had died, then He must have known when he became ill. Be confident that He knows *your* circumstances, even before they happen!

Really? That's all there is to it?

No, there's more, and you will be the major player.

Let me be perfectly honest with you. Most people, will not be able to just "give it to God". We've all heard the expression "*Let go, let God!*" That might work for you, but it has never worked for me. I saw no blessings whatsoever in this calamity that befell my wife, but what God showed me ***during*** this event has changed my life, and I desperately want it to change yours.

Ephesians 6:17 tells us to speak the Word of God as a "*sword of the Spirit*" into situations. The sword, which represents God's word (the Bible) is the only offensive weapon that God says we need; (that and prayer, of course). Hebrews 4:12 expands the thought (and our knowledge) for us: "*For the word of God is living and active and sharper than any two-edged sword and piercing as far as the division of soul and spirit, of both joints and marrow, and able to judge the thoughts and intentions of the heart.*"

The first thing this Scripture tells us about God's word is that it "*is living and active.*" Does this ring a bell for you? Didn't we just read about the tense of Romans 10:17? About "*hearing and hearing*" God's word in the present over and over? God's word is not dated, not out of date, and not historical nor is it meant only for those who lived during the times when it was written. It's meant for the present time of any age and for any people. The word is *active*, which means **"infinite, alive, vigorous and energetic," and *it's in the present tense.***

What does God say about His word? Let's read Proverbs 4: "*My son, give attention to My words; Incline your ear to my sayings. Do not let them depart from your sight; Keep them in the midst of your heart. For they are life to those who find them and health to all their body*" (Prov. 4:20–22).

Wow! Now we're getting somewhere! Every verb in these passages is in the present tense: "give", "incline", "depart", "keep", and finally, the plural present tense of the verb "to be". The fact that these words are still pertinent in our faith almost three thousand years after Proverbs was written, suggests that there is a future element to these present tenses.

But let me share something with you. The biblical Hebrew language has no provision for a future tense in its verb structure. It's all in the present or past tense! That may sound weird until you read the explanation!

Contemporary Jewish commentator Nahum Sarna calls these linguistics of speaking about the future in the past or imperfect tense as "***prophetic perfect***". But pay attention to what he goes on to say, "*The future is described as having already occurred because God's will inherently and ineluctably (inevitably) possesses the power of realization so that the time factor is inconsequential.*"

On this topic of speaking in the past to suggest a future event, I found this excerpt from Marc Saperstein, who in this dissertation presented at Harvard University in 1977, takes an excerpt of his own from Rabbi Isaac ben Yedaiah, a thirteenth century Jewish Rabbi:

> *[The rabbis] of blessed memory followed, in these words of theirs, in the paths of the prophets who speak of something which will happen in the future, in the language of the past. Since they saw in prophetic vision that which was to occur in the future, they spoke about it in the past tense and testified firmly that it had happened, to teach the certainty of his [God's] words—may he be blessed—and his positive promise that can never change and his beneficent message that will not be altered.*

Let's review something we studied in chapter 2 by recalling Isaiah 53:4(a), "*Surely our griefs He himself bore, and our sorrows He carried.*"

Isaiah is speaking about a future event—Christ's actions on the cross—in the past tense (***bore*** and ***carried***). This is a perfect example of "***prophetic perfect***". Because of "*the certainty of his [God's] words—may he be blessed—and his positive promise that can never change and his beneficent message that will not be altered,*" we can claim the healing from all disease and brokenheartedness now and in the future! It is in the past tense to us, because it happened in the past and it appears to be linguistically normal. But remember, it was written for the future as if it had already happened.

Our healing, our rest, our well-being, our prosperity, our joy, our peace all became available when Christ cried, "***It is finished***" in John 19:30. All of it is still available to you (in the future) because it has already happened!

Back to Proverbs 4:20–22: "*My son, give attention to My words; Incline your ear to my sayings. Do not let them depart from your sight; Keep them in the midst of your heart. For they are <u>life</u> to those who find them and <u>health</u> to all their body.*"

Clearly, God wants His words (the Bible) to be heard (***Incline your ear to my sayings***); to be read (***Do not let them depart from your sight***); and finally, to be embraced deep in your innermost being (***Keep them in the midst of your heart***).

Your Part: Step by Step to Enter His Rest

#1 Don't confess unbelief.

The carnal nature of our minds will generally (unless trained) turn to the negative when we are under duress. This becomes the equivalent to confessing "unbelief" when you are trying to enter God's rest. If the glass is always *half* empty in your world, employing a positive attitude becomes *twice* as difficult because you have already set yourself up as a victim. The ensuing stress that flows from a negative attitude will diminish your energy, your attention span, and motivation. If most of your thoughts are negative; that is, if you respond to life with disparaging thoughts instead of uplifting, hopeful thoughts, then you are well on your way to crushing your human spirit.

Whether you are facing illness, financial difficulties or relational issues, you need to exchange habits. Break the habit of thinking negative with a habit of thinking positive. This is important because constant negative thinking has been clinically proven to bring on stress, and stress leads to all kinds of health issues.

When we indulge in negative thinking we unknowingly begin to hypnotize ourselves. The mind is such a powerful tool that repetitive negative thoughts will eventually program itself for failure. We will look deeper into positive thoughts and their effect in the next chapter.

As I drove home from the hospital the night before Janelle's surgery, my head was exploding with negative thoughts: *What if tomorrow morning is the last time we have together? What if she doesn't make it? What if she loses motor skills? What if she loses her speech, her sight?*

Friends, read carefully what I am about to say.

I'm a pastor and I am confessing "unbelief". My whole being was consumed with fear—until God laid on my heart a scripture from James 4:7–8: "Submit therefore to God, resist the devil and he will flee from you. Draw near to God and He will draw near to you. Cleanse your hands, you sinners; and purify your hearts, you double-minded."

From that point on, whenever negative thoughts came into my mind, I simply quoted some Scripture, praised Jesus, and expressed something positive, such as, "Thank you, Lord, for keeping Janelle safe."

I consciously went from confessing unbelief—gloom and doom—to confessing the power, love and grace of God. I had friends and family tell me afterwards that they couldn't believe how calm I was in the waiting room during surgery. I had entered His rest. Folks, if you are worrying; if you can't shake those negative thoughts about your situation, then you are confessing that your faith is weaker than your circumstance, and that your circumstance is greater than God's love for you.

Rather than confessing unbelief, confess success; confess victory! Hebrews 4:16, "Therefore let us draw near with confidence to the throne of grace, so that we may receive mercy and find grace to help in our time of need."

#2 Let rest engage Grace, bringing peace.

As God was preparing to bring a great flood to destroy all the evil on earth and all the ways in which man had devoted himself to negative and perverse thoughts, habits and actions, we read about His reactions in Genesis 6:

> *Then the Lord saw that the wickedness of man was great on the earth, and that every intent of the thoughts of his heart was only evil continually. The Lord was sorry that He had made man on the earth, and He was grieved in His heart. The Lord said, "I will blot out man whom I have created from the face of the land, from man to animals to creeping things and to birds of the sky; for I am sorry that I have made them."* (Gen. 6:5–7)

Very nice, Pastor, but what's that got to do with "rest"? Folks, God wants to do the same to all those negative, pernicious thoughts in your mind that are keeping you from His peace, from His Holiness, from His Rest. He wants all that unbelief washed away! Keep reading in Genesis, verse 8. "*But Noah found favor in the eyes of the Lord.*"

The Hebrew word for *Noah* is ***Noach***, which means—are you ready for this? It means "**Rest**"! The Hebrew and Greek words for *favor* are ***t***^{e}***chinnah*** (*tekh-in-naw*) and ***charis*** both of which mean "**Grace**"!

Literally then, "**Rest found Grace in the eyes of the Lord**."

I want to use a children's joke to make sure you get the closing words in this chapter. Here's the joke; one person speaking to another:

First child: "*Once More and Once Again were in a boat, Once More fell out; who was left?*"

Second child: "*Once Again!*"

First child: "*Once More and Once Again were in a boat, Once More fell out; who was left?*"

Second child: "*Once Again!*"

First child: "*Once More and Once Again were in a boat, Once More fell out; who was left?*"

Second child: "*Once Again!*"

Okay, you get the picture. Now, I want you to apply that concept to this:

When your faith is strong enough to give you rest, *you will find God's Grace surrounding you. That Grace will bring you peace—which will bring you rest*—*which will bring you an awareness of Grace; His Grace will bring you peace—which will bring you rest—which will bring you an awareness of Grace.* Wave after wave of Grace will remove all your doubts and bring you rest.

Remember: Noah found favor. Rest found Grace!

A Summary

You must give up on the phrase that most have been taught: "*God helps those who help themselves.*" Contrary to popular opinion, this phrase is *not* in the Bible. In fact, God helps those who are helpless. As long as you are trying to help yourself, you don't need God's help. If you really want to "help", then put all your resources into "entering His rest."

Hebrews 4 has clear instructions for us: "*For the one who has entered His rest has himself also* ***rested from his works,*** *as God did from His. Therefore let us be diligent to enter that rest*" (Heb. 4:10–11). If we plan to struggle with anything during our crisis, then struggle not with the circumstances, struggle with entering His rest! This admonition was given to the Israelites when they chose not to enter the promised land of milk and honey (easy living). They were unable to unite their faith with the Word of God. We have our faith and we have God's Word. What are we going to do with them? The same as the Hebrew nation and perish in our wilderness?

It is important that we learn to stop striving and discover how to rest. Think of it like this: when you rested in the promise of Jesus and accepted Him as your Redeemer, salvation, His greatest work, was yours. You did nothing except believe. He did everything on the cross. Why would you think all of His other blessings would require more effort from you than what you expended for salvation? Got it? No? Please read the entire chapter again.

13

We Have a Covenant Right to Healing

It has been several years since I heard the phrase, "Many Christians have faith a mile wide and an inch thick." For many of us, we know a little about a lot of biblical topics, but there's not a lot of depth to our knowledge about any specific biblical topic. The cause is simple, really; it's like trying to become an accountant by attending a forty-five minute class once a week that includes a greeting, some music, and, of course, the lesson. Learning takes application, study, and desire. Learning isn't about memorizing; it's about understanding and internalizing, or taking it into your innermost being.

I want to discuss healing in this final chapter. Many of you, reading down the table of contents at the front of the book may have skipped everything preceding this just to get yourself to this chapter because you have a health issue, you have anxiety and you want your body healed. You may be disappointed because there isn't going to be much of a "to-do" list. Rather, you may need to become an inch or two deeper in your spiritual understanding!

I found when I was younger (late thirties) that even though I believed in God, I struggled to put Jesus, His Son into the picture. Being intellectually methodical in my thinking and understanding, "childlike" faith wasn't a concept I dabbled in—ever! Logic, science and proof were preferred in any analysis I undertook. Allow me, then to assume that many of you may lean towards that type of personality, so let's start this discussion *scientifically* to see if we can get a foothold, a base—any traction at all toward obtaining your healing. I'll then close by giving you the biblical reasons why your healing is closer than you think.

Mind over Matter

If you are called on to read a verse during a Bible study, your eyes scan the words and send messages to your brain. The brain, whether it knows the words or not, reaches into its memory and enlists the help of everything it knows about syllables and phonetics, familiarity and prior usage, before sending a message to the voice box, neck muscles, jaw, nasal passages, and mouth to release—out loud—what it has just processed. This is pretty intricate stuff and it all happens in a nanosecond.

In another illustration, let's say you are driving along in your car. Researchers tell us your brain makes twenty to twenty-five decisions every minute as it reacts to events initiated by other drivers, pedestrians or nature (blowing wind, rain, bright sunlight, etc.).

The point I'm trying to make is that your mind is at the helm and controls all of your actions and reactions. Your body obeys what your mind or brain tells it to do. A baseball batter swings at a pitch because his brain told him to. In other words, the body or parts of the body such as a finger, an eye or a limb control nothing. Your arm cannot tell a wrist what to do. Every movement comes from the brain or the mind. ***The mind controls every cell in your body. The flesh doesn't do anything without the mind's involvement***.

Well, that's pretty straight forward and with the exception of involuntary actions, such as a twitch or your heart beating, can we agree that the mind is the workhorse in your life? Then, the inquisitive will ask, "What controls the mind?"

What Controls the Mind?

For the unbeliever, the things that control your mind are everything you have ever put into it. You, in fact, are the sum of all understanding, all knowledge—everything you have ever accepted, and remember, from teachings, readings, television, and radio commentaries—even conversations with friends. In short, man and mankind (other people) are responsible for everything you know, everything you trust in and everything you believe in. It all came from someone else. You are only as smart as the latest technological, scientific, social media, musical, artsy, poetic, Comic Con breakthrough.

Now, I'm not talking about your ability to be creative, to take this vast base of knowledge and create, devise or fashion something else. That's a result of the creativity that God gave to man. But have you ever created something from nothing? Something that doesn't have existing knowledge as part of its base? Unlikely. Knowledge builds on knowledge.

What controls the mind in the believer? Can I come back to that, please? It's a big part of the spiritual aspect of healing so let's keep it all together and for now, concentrate on the physical aspect of the mind controlling the body.

The Power of the Body to Heal

Let's get something out in the open regarding illness or sickness: **Drugs don't heal! They mask!**

- If you cut your finger, ***Aleve*** won't heal the cut. It *will* give you *relief* from the pain.
- If you have diabetes, ***Metformin or insulin*** won't cure the disease, but it will reduce the amount of glucose or sugar in your blood.

- If you have COPD or asthma, ***Inhalers*** won't cure your condition but will relieve your breathing difficulties.

Why then, does the body heal that cut in your finger? That healing comes from your **immune system**. Unless you keep injuring yourself, your immune system will heal that cut. The problem in our overall health issues is that we ***do*** keep injuring ourselves by the way we live and the way we eat. Your condition or disease did not develop overnight. It is the result of years of abusing the immune system. Our lifestyles break down our immunity rather than strengthening it. The world uses pesticides and fertilizers to increase production. We alter the genetic material of organisms (known as GMO) to mutate, insert, or delete certain genes. In most cases, the aim is to introduce a new trait to the plant, which does not occur naturally in the species.

We pollute our air and water supplies. We smoke, chew, do drugs, and disregard regular medical checkups. We overindulge, become obese, and generally speaking, we rely on Big Pharma to bail us out.

If we could only get to a point where we recognize that the body has the inborn or inherent ability to fix things. Medical articles are out there that show evidence of the body's ability to heal itself. It doesn't get a lot of press because of the pharmaceutical presence and lobbying pressures.

The James L. Hall Jr. Center for Mind, Body, and Spirit has this to say on their website:

> *There is increasing evidence that the emotional states and behavioral factors in which mental health professionals specialize, play a critical role in the prevention, onset and progression of disease. Most doctors have noticed that a patient's attitude makes a difference in his or her recovery.* ***Lately, however, the medical community are beginning to realize on a much broader basis, just how much influence the brain can have over the body****. The proof is coming more and more quickly showing that*

> *the physical world and the human mind and soul are linked at the deepest levels, and each one influences the others.*
>
> *Research indicates that almost all visits to primary care physicians are in some way related to mental health. About a third of "medically ill" people have psychological problems expressed as physical symptoms. Another third have illnesses as a result of dysfunctional behavior, such as addiction to alcohol, drugs, chemicals or cigarettes. The final third suffer from physical illnesses in which the cure may be influenced by the state of the patient's mind.*
>
> *Slowly but surely, our nation's health-care system is beginning to pay attention to the power of the mind. In part, that's because researchers continue to provide evidence that the mind is a key player in disease and health.*

Yeah, I know. This is like Kreskin bending a spoon with mind power. But how do you know he didn't?

The only solution for us is to learn how to control these "self-healing" properties in our mind. Our thoughts, feelings, and faith can alter the body's functions or makeup. Psychologists and psychiatrists have proven that negative thinking, depression, apprehension, and anxiety cause damage to the body, while good, positive, happy thoughts such as appreciation, love, and caring stimulate the healing process. Socrates wrote, "***There is no illness of the body apart from the mind.***"

Well, there you are, nonbelievers. Just like you train your biceps in the gym, you can train your mind, likely through meditation, to bring some level of healing to your body. But if you read on, you will see that *believers* will have a head start on you and a much higher success rate.

The News Gets Better

As I have mentioned earlier, *believers* have a *covenant right* to their healing. What does that mean? Well, a covenant is an agreement between two or more parties. In this case, God, through His Son's finished works on the cross, is one party and His people are the other party. In other words, if you believe that Jesus Christ is the Son of God sent to forgive our sins and deliver us into eternal life, then everything else He did on the cross is ours also, because of this New Covenant. It too involves the mind, but **the greater force is the presence of the Holy Spirit**. God has made it very clear in His Word that He wants His children healthy. He even gives us some recipes:

Solomon wrote in Proverbs 17:22 "***A joyful heart is good medicine, but a crushed spirit dries up the bones.***" How close is this Scripture to what the psychologists and psychiatrists said on the prior page?

Earlier in Proverbs 3, he makes things very clear: "*Trust in the Lord with all your heart and do not lean on your own understanding. In all your ways acknowledge Him and He will make your paths straight. Do not be wise in your own eyes; fear the Lord and turn away from evil.* ***It will be healing to your body and refreshment to your bones***" (Prov. 3:5–8; emphasis mine).

As if that isn't clear enough, in the next chapter he writes, "*My son, give attention to My words; incline your ear to My sayings. Do not let them depart from your sight; keep them in the midst of your heart. For they are life to those who find them and health to all their body*" (Prov. 4:20–22).

Jesus Loves Me, This I Know!

Joseph Prince, Senior Pastor at the New Creation Church in Singapore, and author of the book, *The Power of Right Believing*, has an incredibly uplifting story that he shares in the second chapter. The original reference occurs in Cornwall, Judson, and Reid. *Who's Love*

Is It Anyway? Closter, New Jersey: Sharon Publications, 1991, pp 58–59. Bear with me as I quote it verbatim. Please read every word!

> *I heard a story of a minister from Oregon who was assigned to provide counseling in a state mental institution. His first assignment was to a padded cell that housed deranged, barely clothed patients. The stench of human excrement filled the room. He couldn't even talk to the inmates, let alone counsel them—the only responses he got were groans, moans and demonic laughter.*
>
> *Then the Holy Spirit prompted him to sit in the middle of the room and for a full hour sing the famous children's hymn that goes, "**Jesus loves me! This I know, for the Bible tells me so. Little ones to Him belong; they are weak, but He is strong.**" Nothing happened at the end of that first day, but he persisted. For weeks, he would sit and sing the same melody with greater conviction each time: "**Yes, Jesus loves me! Yes, Jesus loves me! Yes, Jesus loves me! The Bible tells me so.**"*
>
> *As the days passed, the patients began singing with him one by one. Amazingly, by the end of the first month, thirty-six of the severely ill patients were transferred from the high-dependency ward to a self-care ward. Within a year, all but two were discharged from the mental institution.*

This is probably the clearest life application of Proverbs 4:20–22 (above) I can give you.

- "*My son, give attention to My words; incline your ear to My sayings.*" The patients were a captive audience. In the beginning, they moaned, groaned and laughed, but in time began singing with the minister. They couldn't have done that unless they had been paying attention and listening.

- "*Do not let them depart from your sight; keep them in the midst of your heart.*" This minister was in their sight, very visible every day. It is likely that these patients began to look forward to his visits, just for the deviation from their dismal hopelessness. They were eager for more. It's obvious that these words were embedded in their heart because they weren't reading music here; they were *reciting* music from their memory, their mind, and their heart!
- "*For they are life to those who find them and health to all their body.*" After one month, thirty-six patients (we're not told how many total patients there were) were transferred from the "*high dependency ward* to a *self-care ward*". I have to think that a high dependency ward doesn't promote much "living". If anything, it wouldn't promote many self-sustaining activities, but rather, many reliance-type activities. On the other hand, a self-care ward sounds like there's a lot more life activities and decisions being made by the patients. "*Life and health*" after thirty days! Wow! A year goes by and "*all but two*" were discharged from the hospital! How awesome is that?

God's word is holy, anointed, and blessed. When we sing His praises and confess Jesus as Lord, we too find health and fullness of life. Asking for His wisdom and understanding every time we open the Bible will expose us to a spiritual awakening beyond anything we can humanly understand.

Using His Word, His Rest, and the Holy Spirit for Healing

As many media commercials tell us, "*But wait, there's more!*" This time there really is! Not only do we have the Word of God to strengthen us, Christ sent us the Holy Spirit to make sure we wouldn't weaken, tire, and fall away. When we combine these two powerful forces with entering His rest, we become darn near infallible. But let me caution you to read the fine print, which says, "*You will be a big part in this.*"

If you want healing in your friend's body, you do what 1 Thessalonians 5:17 tells us to do: "*Pray without ceasing.*" Does this mean pray all the time? Never stop? No, it means that our King has invited us to pray whenever we want. We can come into the holy of holies, come before the Mercy Seat, enter the entire Treasury of Grace whenever we so desire. God is always there. It is never too late or too early. Our King requires no appointment; He is always available to listen to our petitions. We never have to wonder, "*Is this is a good time, Lord?*" There is never a time when we should cease from prayer thinking God needs a break or God is busy just now. Pray without ceasing means ***never abandon prayer! Never assume it isn't God's will! Never quit because you haven't received an answer yet!*** Believe me, God will let you know when He wants you to stop praying about an issue.

Pray without ceasing means ***never leave the Mercy Seat without an answer.*** If you are praying as Jesus might pray (remember I suggested you read the Gospels and take notes of Jesus's proclivities so that you would know His Will) then ***never depart from His Treasury of Grace*** empty-handed because the answer is forthcoming. In all you do as your various days go by, always keep an attitude of prayer to retreat to as events, conversations, and thoughts lead you. In other words, let prayer and the conscious knowledge that Christ is near, be your gravity. Always fall toward prayer, never toward unbelief or defeat.

I use the "*pray without ceasing*" example to show you the difference between praying for someone else's infirmity and dealing with your own. Back in chapter 2, I reflected that Jesus knew when Lazarus had died and suggested to you that He must also have known when Lazarus became ill. It's the same for your ailment. Christ *knows* your condition. He knows you are sick!

Your Illness Was Not Left on the Cross!

Isaiah claims in Isa. 53:4: "*Surely our griefs He Himself bore.*" We don't believe that statement. The Holy Spirit, when prompting Isaiah to write this knew we would struggle with it. That's why Isaiah was instructed to put the word "surely". It refers to the previous verse in that mankind has struggled to hold our Savior in reverence. In fact, many use His name as a cuss word. A great portion of mankind has despised our Lord, not esteemed Him. You may have been one of them until you repented and accepted Him as your Lord. Surely, then means "*and yet*" or "*but*". You wouldn't be wrong to read verse 3 and then say, "*Despite all of this...*" It is meant to show all mankind the depth of His forgiveness and love.

Earlier in this book, I explained that *griefs* was translated as ***illness, sickness, and disease.*** Let's take a closer look at the words, "*He Himself bore.*" In the Hebrew, Vulgate and Septuagint versions, the sense is that of sustaining, bearing, upholding, or carrying as when one removes a burden from the shoulders of one and places it on his own. It means to take up, to lift, to raise, to bear or to carry as a tree bears its fruit. Eerily similar to His utterance, "*I am the vine, you are the branches*" (John 15:5). The verse goes on to say, "*He who abides in Me and I in him, he bears much fruit, for apart from Me you can do nothing.*" I love the double entendre. In relation to doing good works, if we are in Christ and He is in us, we can't help but bear rewarding and fulfilling fruit or works. In relation to healing, He implies, "*I am the vine; I am bearing the weight, I am carrying your burdens; your job is to rest and bear fruit.*" If we refuse to acknowledge that He has borne, lifted up or carried off our diseases, then He accurately predicts our fate: "*Apart from Me you can do nothing.*"

This idea of lifting up from us, sustaining, and carrying away does not imply that Our Lord became diseased just as it does not indicate that when He took our sins, He became sinful. It is an act of removal accomplished solely by His power, His will, and His Grace. We can also have our sicknesses lifted from us, carried away, and be restored to wholeness.

Lifted Up, Carried Away

Exactly one year to the date of Janelle's brain surgery where one of the two brain bleeds was closed off and repaired, she went for a follow-up MRI. The surgeon reviewed the results and told us that everything was fine. "Would you like to see the area we operated on," he asked? "The images didn't mean a lot to us, just that there was only the tiniest of scars where he had repaired her bleed. I said to him, "What does the other bleed look like?"

We had trusted God all year that the second bleed area would not become a problem, but we never forgot about it. You see, the surgeon was unable to get to that bleed because of the dense nerve network in the brain stem between the first bleed and that area.

He scrolled through many "slices" of Janelle's brain looking for the second bleed. Finally, he said, "I can't see it; it's not there anymore!" Carried away. Healed through the love and grace of Jesus.

I referred (chapter 1) to mankind's monumental "flip-flop" since New Testament times when they routinely flocked to Christ to be healed but the religious order thought He was blaspheming when He talked about forgiving sin. Today, it's just the opposite. We relish in the knowledge that our sins are forgiven, and we are going to spend eternity in heaven. But if the doctor tells you that you have cancer, high anxiety, terror, and alarm grips and controls your entire being. The news takes over your life; you have no direction, everything about life now centers around your condition. It becomes difficult to gather your thoughts. Throughout the day, you are consumed with your new reality. You wake in the morning and the dread hits you like a blast from a hot oven.

Spiritual Brainwashing

How can we get past this? The first thing we need to do is realize that healing is still available today, through Christ. What He did on the cross never expires, is never restricted to "*someone else*" and is never insufficient for our illness.

Let's look at it this way. Some of the things you might say in various situations regarding your salvation would be:

- "*I know I'm going to heaven when I die.*"
- "*We'll see him/her again in heaven.*"
- "*I'm so thankful so-and-so led me to the Lord.*"
- "*We are heavenly beings trapped in an earthly body.*"

In other words, we never express doubt as to our final resting place. Why? Because Christ assured us that He would go and prepare a place for us (John 14:3). It is the very cornerstone of our faith. Yet in Isaiah's prophecy, it came second after Christ lifted up and carried away our diseases. We should be walking around confessing healing:

- "*I can't wait to see the look on the doctor's face when he can't find the tumors.*"
- "*I don't know when, but I do know I am in the process of being healed.*"
- "*Why should I worry? Christ already lifted this illness from me.*"
- "*I feel the pain Lord, but I know the healing has already started.*"

This is exactly what we should be doing. First of all, we confess the completed works of Christ on the cross. He ***did*** lift and carry away ***all*** sicknesses and diseases! That gives us the covenant right to healing. Don't pray for it—it has already occurred. We just need to manifest it into our body. By praying for it, you are telling God that what Christ did on the cross wasn't enough; you need Him to heal *your* illness.

I started all of this by referring to science—mind over matter. All science is put in place by God. Therefore, we can also employ some of this science in our healing.

It is critical in our healing process to see ourselves the way God sees us. Let me ask you a question: "When God looks at you, does He see your sin?" If you answered yes, I have to refer you to 2 Corinthians 5:21, which states, "*He made Him who knew no sin to be sin on our behalf, so that we might become the righteousness of God in*

Him." What does it mean to be the righteousness of God in Christ Jesus? It simply means that when God looks at us, He sees us through Jesus Christ and His finished work of the cross. We are completely accepted by God and are clothed with Jesus's robes of righteousness.

By the same measure, when God looks at us He does not see our illness. He sees us fully whole, fully restored—once again through Christ. It doesn't mean He isn't aware of our sickness, just like He is aware of our sin (until we confess it). It simply means He sees us restored, healthy, and vibrant. It's not the way you feel, I know, but it is the way God sees you. We need to see ourselves as God sees us. We need to confess healing, wholeness, and restoration *without ceasing.*

Bringing the mind back into play, when our thoughts are negative and contrary to God's seeing and doing, *we will be defeated!* On the other hand, when we line up our thoughts and beliefs with God, our breakthrough is imminent! It has to be! He is not a God of destruction. His thoughts are pure, wholesome, and restorative. His thoughts will heal, prosper, and mend your relationships. But you must see yourself as He does. Consider this: If Christ suffered on the cross as we know He did, then is it just that God would put you through the same suffering? Remember the "***Invariable Principle of Justice***" I mentioned back? If I'm going to suffer with my affliction, why then did Christ suffer for the same affliction? Was His suffering not enough?

Immunity and Renewal

Barbara German of Epic Journey Ministries said it this way, by incorporating our immune system into the discussion:

> *Wow… I like this image of our faith being like our immune system… I can relate to that concept… I recognize how important my immune system is to my body's health in the natural realm and how there are things I can do which either support/help or hin-*

der its ability to do its work in my body... Oh, how FAITH is important to my soul...

IF I regularly do those things which takes the measure of faith Jesus has given me and grow that faith, then my thoughts, my emotions and my will are naturally strengthened and encouraged to be aligned with God's and that becomes a powerful immune boost against the wiles of the enemy!

HOW do I do this? By RENEWING my mind... by reading God's Word and spending time in His presence...

When we do this, the spirit of God within us resonates with truth... there is a stirring that gets the attention of our soul (our mind, our will, and our emotions) and then finally, every cell within our body hears the truth & lines up... this brings transformation to every cell, every ounce of our being!"

"Transformation to every cell which lines up in agreement." How? By renewing our mind! **I will be healed because Christ provided.** The Holy Spirit is unleashed to deliver healing to every cell in our body!

The Role of the Holy Spirit

Remember, the mind controls every aspect of our body. I asked the question earlier (and made you wait for the answer) "What controls the mind?" In believers, it is the Holy Spirit! He is our direct link, our only conduit to God. If you ask for wisdom as Solomon did, God will deliver it directly to your mind through the Holy Spirit. If you stumble over prayer, the Holy Spirit will interpret your deepest groans—the ones you can't quite find the words for—and transmit them directly to God. If you seek healing, the Holy Spirit will direct you to verses that renew your mind and keep you from confessing unbelief.

I love Jeremiah 32:27, "*Behold, I am the Lord! The God of all flesh! Is anything too difficult for Me?*" Your only role in all of this is renewing your mind, being in the word, entering His rest, and confessing the truth about Christ's finished works on the cross. The part of the Holy Spirit in all of this is multifaceted. The Bible declares that the Holy Spirit is *the power of God* (2 Tim. 1:7), that it *leads us into all truth* (John 14:17, 26), that it enables us to *discern spiritual things* (1 Cor. 2:10–14).

As we search the Bible, we will find that the Holy Spirit is the *nature, power, and essence* of God. It is also a gift that God can impart to a human mind to promote and inspire spiritual growth.

The *Nature* of God is creativity, vibrancy, and wholeness. The *Power* of God is healing and restoration. The *Essence* of God is all things good. In His essence, there is no room for decay, sickness, or depression. The Holy Spirit in you will deliver your healing, will deliver your prosperity if you are in financial difficulties, and will deliver restored relationships if there are issues with you and your family members or coworkers. But you must see yourself as God sees you and confess restoration, not unbelief!

There's a Battle Going On for Control of Your Mind

First Peter 5:8 tells us, "*Be of sober spirit, be on the alert. Your adversary, the devil, prowls around like a roaring lion, seeking someone to devour.*" This Scripture should send a message loud and clear to every Christian: Satan **cannot sneak up on you!** Could a roaring lion sneak up on you? He *will* come against you, however. He'll try to control your thoughts and emotions. If you get that cancer scare, he will bring gloom and despair into your feelings. Please remember, Christ already defeated this enemy! Don't let these reactions lead to unbelief.

Expressing the truths about God's word, the power of the Holy Spirit, and the finished works of Christ on the cross will bring you grace and blessings. And… Satan will flee! (James 4:7). No matter how cunning Satan gets in his attempt to control your mind, it is your emotions that will bring you results. If Satan gets to you, you will be fearful and anxious. If you dwell on God's word and the power of the Holy Spirit your emotions will turn to upbeat, positive thoughts.

Your healing will not begin in your flesh, it will begin in your mind. Many times in Scripture, Christ referred to the depth of someone's faith. Paraphrasing, He said often, "*It is done according to your faith.*" Hebrews 11:1 says, "*Now faith is the assurance of things hoped for, the conviction of things not seen.*" Also, let's consider 2 Corinthians 10:3–5, "*For though we walk in the flesh, we do not war according to the flesh, for the weapons of our warfare are not of the flesh, but divinely powerful for the destruction of fortresses. We are destroying speculations and every lofty thing raised up against the knowledge of God, and we are taking every thought captive to the obedience of Christ.*"

Keeping the word of God ever-present in our mind keeps us in control of our mind and when we have control of our mind, we have control of our body—every single cell! Remember, not every thought in your mind comes from you! Become alert to recognizing those thoughts that need to be taken captive through Christ, and you will begin to see your healing.

Your Complete Well-Being

Because we worship a God of Love, a God of Grace, and a God of Righteousness, we have to believe that He did not lay all of mankind's sin on Christ at the cross to see His Son suffer. Neither did He burden our Savior with every disease and sickness known to man so that Christ would decay. In fact, He did all of these things so that we would be free from all of these issues. If God didn't want to heal His children, why did He burden Christ with disease? If you were meant to suffer, why did Christ also have to suffer?

Your complete well-being was assured and paid for by Christ's finished works on the cross. This book is primarily a book of prayer. That was my intention when I began to write it. However, God showed me that your peace of mind, your well-being are also vitally important to Him. Perhaps He has a hard time envisioning His people spreading the Gospel to all the world if they are broken, worried and anxious about disease in their body; if they are restricted severely by financial hardship or if they lack fulfillment with family because of ill-will and prior events. In this last addendum for you, pray and take into your understanding the last seven words. They will be vital to your wholeness.

Remember how powerful the mind is. This is how the Holy Spirit delivers healing—through the mind. The mind controls every cell in your body. Don't ask for healing, instead thank God for it. ***Prayer is more about receiving than asking.***

NOTES

1. Pastor Jerry Dickinson of the West Side Church of God in Glendale, Arizona.
2. Charles Swindoll, *Living Above the Level of Mediocrity* (Thomas Nelson, 1990), 225.
3. Dutch Sheets, *Intercessory Prayer* (Regal from Gospel Light, 1996).
4. Ibid.
5. Ibid.
6. Jim Cymbala, *The Life God Blesses* (Zondervan, 2001).
7. Dutch Sheets, *Intercessory Prayer* (Regal from Gospel Light), 208
8. Ronald Dunn, *Don't Just Stand There, Pray Something* (Thomas Nelson Publishers), 171.
9. PeRPs - Professional Religious People.
10. Joel Preston, "Sermons on Unbelief," Sermoncentral.com, May 2012.
11. *The New Strong's Expanded Dictionary of Bible Words* (Thomas Nelson Publishers, 2001), 305.
12. Ibid., 739 of the Hebrew translations.
13. Ibid., 1217 of the Greek translations.
14. Jentezen Franklin, *The Amazing Discernment of Women.*
15. *The New Strong's Expanded Dictionary of Bible Words* (Thomas Nelson Publishers, 2001), 1249 of the Greek translations.
16. C. H. Spurgeon, sermon #1051, May 19, 1872; a sermon delivered at the Metropolitan Tabernacle, Newington.
17. J. R. Miller, written in 1888.

ABOUT THE AUTHOR

Pastor Clark has worked in, studied, taught, and basically observed the human condition in eight different countries around the world covering Western, European, and Far Eastern civilizations. People all over the world, he found, gravitate to and rely on a *higher power* from time to time.

After many discussions, he found that people's expectations in their dealings with their deities were directly proportional to the depth of their belief or faith in those deities.

I wrote *Jesus Wept*, he says, to show Christians how very much our God loves them and why it is safe to believe and hope deeply. This book will show them that it isn't up to God to do what they are praying for—He's already done everything on the cross; it's up to the petitioner to accept what has already been done.